PAUL SIMON
SIMON & GARFUNKEL

BY CHRIS CHARLESWORTH

Copyright © 1997 Omnibus Press
(A Division of Book Sales Limited)

Cover & Book designed by 4i
Picture research by Nikki Russell

ISBN 0.7119.5597.2 Order No.OP47829

Exclusive Distributors:
Book Sales Limited, 8/9 Frith Street, London W1V 5TZ, UK.
Music Sales Corporation, 257 Park Avenue South, New York, NY 10010, USA.
Music Sales Pty Limited, 120 Rothschild Avenue, Rosebery, NSW 2018, Australia.

To the Music Trade only:
Music Sales Limited, 8/9 Frith Street, London W1V 5TZ, UK.

Photo credits:
Front Cover: London Features International;
Other pictures supplied by Harry Goodwin, LFI, Barry Plummer & Rex Features.
Every effort has been made to trace the copyright holders of the photographs in this book but one or
two were unreachable. We would be grateful if the photographers concerned would contact us.

Printed in the United Kingdom by Ebenezer Baylis & Son, Worcester.

A catalogue record for this book is available from the British Library.

OMNIBUS PRESS
LONDON · NEW YORK · SYDNEY

CONTENTS

INTRODUCTION

"I tend not to be sloppy," Paul Simon told me in 1975, in a characteristically measured response to my suggestion that he was popular music's greatest perfectionist. Understatement is as much a hallmark of Simon's music as the precision he brings to his work, and his deliberately low-key *modus operandi* nurtures the now accepted image of a quiet, uncharismatic craftsman treading the fine line between commercial acceptance, musical innovation and his own scrupulous standards.

Paul Simon is by no means prolific. In over 30 years he has recorded only around 150 songs; about a third of them with his former partner, the singer Art Garfunkel, the rest as a solo performer. This averages out at less than five compositions a year, and since the vast majority of these were recorded between 1965 and 1975, his output over the past two decades has been miserly to say the least. Indeed, the last ten years has seen the release of just two new Simon albums, the stunning *Graceland* and its successor *Rhythm Of The Saints*, together with a live set recorded at his

1991 concert in New York's Central Park.

Paul Simon's work is spread over four separate and quite distinct careers in music. The first, thankfully brief, was as one half (with Art Garfunkel) of Tom & Jerry, a now forgotten be-bop duo; clean, crew-cut, tie-wearing types who had one very minor hit, 'Hey Schoolgirl', and who recorded one album which is no longer available and, as long as Simon has his way, likely to remain so.

Five years later the same pair re-emerged after a shaky start as the markedly different Simon & Garfunkel, who looked like thoughtful college boys and sang with a purity envied by everyone in class. Polite, well-educated and as solemn as they were inscrutable, S&G were among the most popular acts of the Sixties, and for all his trying Paul Simon has never quite managed to shake off their legacy. Simon, of course, was far and away the dominant partner, writing virtually all their material, singing and providing acoustic guitar back-up that was as skilled as any finger picker in the world. Garfunkel confined himself to the outstanding high vocal harmonies and the occasional epic solo performance. The production of S&G records, generally attributed to engineer Roy Halee and Simon himself, set industry standards in clarity and quality, and many of their best known songs have become popular standards, heard in elevators and airport lounges, eternally hummed on the unconscious breath.

The partnership dissolved amid some rancour in 1970 after the release of *Bridge Over Troubled Water*, an album which sold upwards of nine million copies world-wide, then a landmark in record industry sales figures. As if relieved to be on his own at last Simon sat back to enjoy the royalties that *Bridge* brought him before carefully embarking on what was soon to become an auspicious solo career, recording six fairly eclectic and well received albums with varying degrees of artistic and commercial success until 1983 when, with sales figures declining, he seemed to be heading up a cul-de-sac. So Simon stepped back, reconsidered his goals, found fresh inspiration and re-launched himself three years later on what has been the most triumphant phase of his entire career.

Graceland, released in 1986, was Simon's masterpiece, an artistic triumph, which in hindsight had been on the cards since he and Garfunkel recorded 'El Condor Pasa', a Peruvian folk song, for the *Bridge* album 16 years earlier. In his solo work, Simon had become increasingly fascinated by third world musics and rhythms, and on *Graceland* he finally abandoned all trace of his earlier folk style and tin-pan alley singer-songwriter background for an all out album of music influenced by the sounds of Soweto. Finally, it seemed, he'd thrown off the 'formerly of Simon & Garfunkel' tag, even if he does occasionally bow to audience demand in concert and, as a final encore, wearily welcome back his old friend the darkness.

"I'm not a jukebox," Paul Simon observed somewhat testily from the stage of London's Royal Albert Hall some years ago in response to audience requests for his golden oldies. In a career that now spans over thirty years, he's earned the right to ignore such demands and do exactly as he likes, and at the time of writing he is reported to be working on a stage musical, thus realising a long held ambition. Like all the greatest pop writers, he is unwilling to rest on his laurels and is continually searching for new territories to explore. That's what keeps him fresh – and what sets him apart from so many lesser talents who emerged in the singer-songwriter boom of the late Sixties and early Seventies. In not being sloppy, he's reached a class of his own.

I am grateful to Patrick Humphries for his assistance in researching this book. Considering his record sales and critical acclaim, Paul Simon has attracted surprisingly little attention as far as literary works are concerned, but Patrick's Paul Simon biography *The Boy In The Bubble* (Sidgwick & Jackson, 1988) was particularly useful, as were *Simon & Garfunkel: The Definitive Biography* by Victoria Kingston (Sidgwick & Jackson, 1996) and *Paul Simon Now And Then* by Spencer Leigh (Raven Books, 1973). Thanks also to Chris Allen, especially for his thoughts on *Graceland*, Andrew King and Dave McAleer.

Chris Charlesworth, 1996

THE EARLY RECORDINGS

The common perception that Simon & Garfunkel emerged from nowhere as overnight successes to enjoy a number one hit with their first ever single belies the lengthy musical apprenticeship that Simon, at least, underwent before *Billboard* magazine showed 'The Sound Of Silence' at the top of its charts in December of 1965.

In the beginning, as Tom And Jerry, Paul Simon and Art Garfunkel were neighbourhood friends and pop music nuts from the New York suburb of Queens, who hustled their way into making a single for the independent Big label in 1957. It was called 'Hey Schoolgirl' and it reached number 54 in the US. It is difficult now to reconcile the chorus of this song – "Hey-bop-a-loo-chi-bop" – with the man who would later write songs with the depth of 'Bridge Over Troubled Water', the imagery of 'Renée And Georgette Magritte With Their Dog After The War' or the originality of 'The Boy In The Bubble', but everybody has to start somewhere. According to most accounts, 'Hey Schoolgirl' was followed by a Tom & Jerry album which sank like a stone and which, like the single, was not released in the UK. The existence of this album in 1957 cannot be confirmed, but in 1967 Pickwick Records in the UK either re-issued it, or created an album by compiling various Tom & Jerry tracks together, with a misleading contemporary photograph, and added liner notes suggesting that this was S&G's crucial early roots. Simon, aware that a con was being perpetrated, promptly injuncted it and it has remained officially unavailable ever since.

After Tom and Jerry, Simon continued to hang around New York's pop Mecca, the Brill Building, where his offices are now situated, and made records for various small independent labels (Big, Warwick, Madison, Amy) under the pseudonym Jerry Landis and with a studio band who called themselves Tico and The Triumphs. He also used the name True Taylor on a rockabilly single which sounds remarkably unlike Paul Simon. Again, none of these recordings are currently available, though with a little diligence they can be found on bootleg by anyone who is sufficiently interested to seek them out.

Many of these recordings are very similar in structure, based around either the classic doo-wop style made famous by Frankie Lymon & The Teenagers and Dion & The Belmonts, or the common I-VI-IV-V (in the key of C, the chords C, Am, F and G) ballad progression utilised, for example, in Marty Wilde's well known UK pop hit 'Donna' or The Beatles' 'This Boy'. The influence of The Everly Brothers, Dion, Buddy Holly and, occasionally, Elvis Presley, is easy to spot. All of them are typical of their era, the late Fifties, when pop was taking over from rock and sharp entrepreneurs were using

pop music to play on the tender emotions of impressionable teenage girls. It's likely that many of the ballads were written in the hope that they might be recorded by the bland teen idols of the day, singers like Frankie Avalon, Fabian and Bobby Vee.

Although much of this early material might seem very trivial by the standards of Paul Simon's later work, it would be a mistake to dismiss it too lightly. This was Simon's musical kindergarten, his equivalent of The Beatles in Hamburg, and as he hung around the small studios, record company offices and the Brill Building, as he listened to everything that was going on around him, he learned his trade, the lessons that would stand him in good stead for years to come. He learned how songs are constructed, what is commercial, what is trite and what is acceptable. (He also learned about how the music business worked and how to survive within it, which probably explains why – unlike so many of his contemporaries – Paul Simon has never been involved in ugly litigation over copyright ownership through having signed unpropitious contracts early in his life.)

Unlikely as it may now seem, these songs and the circumstances in which they were recorded, were the foundations on which Paul Simon built his career, and since that career has now lasted almost 40 years and shows no sign of flagging, it is safe to say that these were very valuable lessons indeed.

Known Tom & Jerry, Jerry Landis, Tico & The Triumphs and True Taylor recordings are as follows:

Hey Schoolgirl/(T&J): A doo-wop workout with snappy chord changes similar to The Everly Brothers' 'Wake Up Little Susie'.

Dancing Wild/(T&J): B-side of the above, and very similar in style.

True or False/(TT): Rockabilly effort, drawled in a Deep South accent.

Teenage Fool/(TT): An echo-laden rockabilly ballad not unlike the slower recordings made by Elvis during his Sun sessions.

Our Song/(T&J): Everly Brothers rockabilly style work-out with a neat guitar solo, all about their favourite song on the jukebox.

Two Teenagers/(T&J): Dreadfully camp moon-in-June doo-wop number featuring high-pitched girl chorus chirping "So in love" after the title.

(Pretty Baby) Don't Say Goodbye/(T&J): Naïve sentimental song rhyming 'cry' with 'goodbye' on the choruses, with Everly Brothers style harmonies.

That's My Story/(T&G): Primarily Art wallowing in a I-VI-IV-V style doo-wop ballad.

Baby Talk/(T&G): Classic doo-wop rock song written by Jan and Dean, recorded in the style of Johnny Cymbal's 'Mr Bass Man'. Great fun.

Anna Belle/(JL): A hot rock'n'roll number sung by Paul in the style of Buddy Holly.

Loneliness/(JL): Maudlin ballad.

Swanee/(JL): Cover of well known minstrel/Al Jolson hit by Caesar-Gershwin, *c*. 1920.

Toot Toot Tootsie Goodbye/(JL): B-side of above, also Al Jolson cover, by Gus Kahn, original *c*. 1922.

I'd Like To Be The Lipstick On Your Lips/(JL): Teen ballad but don't blame

Paul Simon for the title – he didn't write it.

Just A Boy/(JL): Limp teen ballad.

Play Me A Sad Song/(JL): Soul crooning pop.

It Means A Lot To Them/ (JL): Generation gap teen ballad.

Ask Me Why/(JL): Undistinguished romantic I-VI-IV-V style ballad.

I'm Lonely/(JL): Shades of future alienation songs on this moody ballad.

I Wish I Weren't In Love/(JL): Nightmarishly bad lyrics on a sentimental doo-wop ballad bemoaning the horrors of unrequited love.

Motorcycle/(T&TT): Stunningly original rock'n'roll tribute to two-wheeled hot rods, punctuated by the sounds of engines roaring and the kind of doo-wop harmonies that enhanced The Beach Boys' best car songs. Tico rasps the lyrics.

I Don't Believe Them/(T&TT): Slow I-VI-IV-V style ballad.

Wildflower/(T&TT): Bo Diddley beat-style rocker whose Spanish lyrics give it a Mexican slant.

Express Train/(T&TT): Train sounds introduce a Dion & The Belmonts style rocker with 'clickety-clickety' lyrics.

Get Up And Do The Wobble/(T&TT): Typical dance track of the era; Simon's take on Little Eva's smash hit 'The Locomotion'.

Cry Little Boy Cry/(T&TT): Dull slab of melancholia with Dion style slow start.

The Lone Teen Ranger/(JL): Hilarious novelty send-up of *The Lone Ranger* TV show in which Jerry bemoans the loss of his girl to the masked Teen Ranger! Complete with pistol shots, 'Hi-Ho Silver' lyrics and Rossini's *William Tell* overture! Probably inspired by The Olympics' 1958 hit 'Western Movies'.

Lisa/(JL): Soft I-VI-IV-V style ballad in which Jerry sends a 'Dear John' letter to the unfortunate Lisa because he's not yet ready to settle down.

Noise/(T&TT): A rocking doo-wop effort about a party where the guests made lots of noise!

Cards Of Love/(T&TT): Shang-a-lang doo-wop song with lyrics based on the pack of cards – "You were my Queen, I was your King, then Jack stole you". Ouch!

Fighting Mad/(T&J): Everly Brothers style rocker.

Surrender Please Surrender/(T&J): The Everly Brothers meet Buddy Holly on this ballad, with changes not unlike Holly's 'Everyday'.

Looking At You/(T&J): A fast tempo rock'n'roller.

I'm Lonesome/(T&J): Typically slowish I-VI-IV-V style ballad of which hundreds were recorded between 1958 and 1962.

Note: Two instrumentals, 'Simon Says' and 'Tijuana Blues', were also included on the Tom and Jerry LP.

WEDNESDAY MORNING, 3AM

exciting new sounds in the folk tradition by

SIMON & GARFUNKEL

SIMON & GARFUNKEL

WEDNESDAY MORNING, 3AM

ORIGINAL UK ISSUE: CBS 63370, OCTOBER 1968; ORIGINAL US ISSUE: COLUMBIA 9049,
APRIL 1964; CURRENT CD: COLUMBIA 463375-2

After the false start that was Tom & Jerry and their immediate successors, both Simon & Garfunkel went to college, but Paul Simon was never likely to drop music from his agenda. He studied English literature and, briefly, law, and went on a pilgrimage to Europe, stopping for a while in Paris before settling for several months in London where he played guitar and sang in folk clubs, and wrote many of his best early songs. He returned to America in mid-1964 and performed at various folk clubs in New York's Greenwich Village, occasionally with Garfunkel.

With Bob Dylan then leading a huge folk revival in New York, it was a particularly advantageous time to be on the boards in the Village, and Simon soon attracted favourable attention. He might have lacked the street cred of many of his peers but he was already a very skilled acoustic guitar player – far better than almost all his contemporaries – and Garfunkel, when he was around, had a voice like a choirboy. And then there were the songs...

It was Simon's anti-racist song 'He Was My Brother' that first attracted the attention of CBS producer Tom Wilson who proposed he make an album for the label with engineer Roy Halee. Simon suggested that Garfunkel sing with him and Wilson acquiesced.

The first album that Simon &

Garfunkel recorded under their own names was a very tentative affair, with only six of Simon's original songs among the largely straight folk material. It is this material that lets the album down, which suggests that Simon ought to have been given a freer rein by his label and casts doubts on the wisdom of CBS in aiming S&G's début album primarily at the folk – as opposed to pop – market. Initial sales were very low – 3,000 copies has been suggested – and when the dust had settled neither S&G nor the label seemed in any great hurry to record a follow-up. Garfunkel went back to college to study architecture, probably thinking his musical career was over, and Simon went back to England.

Although this album was issued in 1964 in the US, it wasn't until four years later, after the success of 'Bookends' and the high profile that Simon & Garfunkel enjoyed as a result of their work on *The Graduate* soundtrack, that CBS decided to release it in the UK. The cover depicts Paul and Art wrapped in college scarves, looking appropriately

thoughtful as they ride a New York subway train.

YOU CAN TELL THE WORLD

Simon & Garfunkel introduce themselves to the world with a joyous gospel track sung with plenty of naïve enthusiasm but lacking real depth or subtlety. The rather academic approach that S&G brought to their music was unlikely to benefit a gospel song that was generally delivered with unfettered enthusiasm by black choirs immersed in the glory of the Lord. The most impressive feature is Simon's rhythmic guitar work, an early example of his strength as an accompanist, not just with precise, claw-hammer finger picking but with confident chord work as well.

LAST NIGHT I HAD THE STRANGEST DREAM

Ed McCurdy's folk standard and his best known song, lacks emotion on this outing but is sung with confidence and, as would become common with S&G,

taste and professionalism. The banjo accompaniment is uncredited but is probably Simon.

Born in Pennsylvania in 1911, McCurdy began his career broadcasting on Canadian radio but moved to New York in the mid-Fifties. Very much a traditionalist and blessed with a pure baritone, in the early Sixties McCurdy emceed jam sessions at the Bitter End in Greenwich Village, which is probably where he crossed paths with Paul Simon.

BLEECKER STREET

Jerry Landis' 'I'm Lonely' aside, 'Bleecker Street' is the earliest recorded example of Simon writing about alienation, a topic that they would sing about to the point of pre-occupation during the coming years. Bleecker Street cuts Greenwich Village from East to West and is the street where most of its music clubs are located, but the song is not so much about the street as the people who inhabit it, the crowds rushing past without communicating with each other.

Slightly clumsy in its manifestation here, Paul Simon would refine the subject as a major theme for his music, eventually making it an art form in itself. Nevertheless, S&G's voices blend together beautifully on the first Simon composition to appear on the album.

SPARROW

'Sparrow', the second Simon original, offers another opportunity to hear how S&G's voices could blend together in a delicate, impeccable harmony that few other ensemble singers would rival. Here Simon utilises the children's rhyme, along with slightly clumsy biblical imagery, to castigate society for its harsh treatment of the weaker souls. The same theme would re-occur in far more sophisticated form, both lyrically and musically, on 'The Boxer' six years later.

BENEDICTUS

A somewhat formal interpretation of a Latin hymn taken from a 16th Century church mass by Orlando de Lasso. Art discovered the song while studying music at Columbia University, and Paul worked out an arrangement for two-part harmony. Curiously conventional and somewhat contrary to Simon's atheistic leanings, this is rather at odds with the more free-spirited work of their Greenwich Village peers.

THE SOUND OF SILENCE

'The Sound Of Silence' is Paul Simon's first major work, although in this first incarnation Garfunkel's vocal purity somehow takes the edge off the frustration that Simon is trying to communicate. A more desperate reading might have conveyed the message better.

Although there's a hint of it on 'Bleecker Street' elsewhere on this album, the thread of loneliness and alienation that runs through so much of Simon's work really begins here. It was

the first song of his to become a hit, a blockbuster number one in fact, and it is still requested whenever he steps on stage. It can be lonely in the city, intones Simon; crowds follow each other like sheep; human relationships are deteriorating in the age of mass communication, of television and telephones. Slow down, Simon seems to be saying, slow down and communicate with one another, and then, only then, will we be saved from this by-product of 20th Century technology.

It seems strange now that no-one recognised this song's hit potential when it was recorded and released in this version. In 1964, it was perhaps just a shade too early for what was essentially a pop song to be taken seriously, even though Dylan was already hammering at the gates of serious critical appraisal. Its time would come.

There have been countless versions of this song released by Simon over the years and the fact that he is willing to return to it in concert years down the line seems to indicate that he retains an

affection for it even now. He even closed his boxed set (see below) with a moving live performance, chosen as the final encore at his concert in Central Park in 1991.

HE WAS MY BROTHER

This was the song that attracted the attention of CBS producer Tom Wilson, who wanted to record it with another folk group he'd signed, and it has been referred to by Simon himself as his first 'serious song'. It was clearly written in sympathy for a human rights demonstrator, apparently killed by the Ku Klux Klan, but the identity of the victim remains unknown. Suggestions that it was written for a former university classmate, Andrew Goodman, who was murdered by the KKK in June 1964 (along with Michael Schwerner and James Chaney) are wide of the mark since Garfunkel has recalled that Simon first played it to him in 1963.

Nevertheless, the song marked Simon's graduation from teenage

romancer to topical singer, although he would never assume the mantle of protest singer in the manner of Dylan, Phil Ochs *et al*. S&G's reading of this folk-styled song seems almost too earnest, but this befitted the subject and reflected the seriousness which Simon felt the song deserved.

PEGGY-O

The traditional folk song, much favoured by unaccompanied folk groups which was also covered by Bob Dylan – as 'Pretty Peggy-O' – on his début album, is given a deferential, albeit rather syrupy, treatment by S&G. Dispensable. The writer is unknown.

GO TELL IT ON THE MOUNTAIN

This traditional American spiritual is sung with plenty of enthusiasm in the rousing style that was typical of Fifties folk singers, but Simon & Garfunkel again add little to the standard arrangement.

Like their version of 'You Can Tell The World', this folk club favourite needs more passion than white graduate students from Queens are likely to muster up.

This song is believed to have been written around 1865, but the composer is unknown.

THE SUN IS BURNING

Another rather luke-warm stab, this time on Ian Campbell's now standard folk song, much favoured by Irish folk singers, including the redoubtable Mary O'Hara. Simon probably encountered the song in England during his first visit to the country.

THE TIMES THEY ARE A-CHANGIN'

Anger is an essential fashion accessory for young men of a certain age, especially songwriters with serious intent, but S&G seemed unable to summon up the required emotion, and nowhere was this more evident than on this straight interpretation of one of Bob Dylan's greatest early songs. This rather tepid rendering added absolutely nothing to the original and, on hearing it, Bob can't have been too worried about the competition from this quarter.

WEDNESDAY MORNING, 3AM

The title song, and the final Simon original, sees the duo relating the tale of a petty liquor store hold-up, but the tension that should visit a song that echoes misery and squalor is lost in the reverence that S&G's pure harmonies bring to the track. There is a mild touch of eroticism as the haunted man watches over the rising breasts of the sleeping woman, but again the effect is lost by the arrangement.

Re-written, and retitled 'Somewhere They Can't Find Me', this song benefited from its harsher treatment on the 'Sounds Of Silence' album.

SOUNDS OF SILENCE

ORIGINAL UK ISSUE, CBS 62690, APRIL 1966; ORIGINAL US RELEASE; COLUMBIA 9269, MARCH 1966; CURRENT CD: COLUMBIA 460954-2

Wednesday Morning 3am turned out to be Simon & Garfunkel's second false start. Back in the UK, Simon again travelled around the folk circuit, making friends among fellow performers and writing more and more songs. Indeed, he appears to have been far more prolific in the UK than back home, as least during this early period. One night he found himself on Widnes railway station, longing to return to London to his girlfriend Kathy. His thoughts became 'Homeward Bound'. Kathy was evidently an important muse, an almost tangible presence in his early love songs.

He was fortunate to befriend Judith Piepe, whose home was a refuge for folk singers and who unstintingly championed them all. Thanks to Judith he recorded 12 songs for BBC radio which, because they fitted in nowhere else, were subsequently broadcast over two weeks on the daily religious programme *Five To Ten*. Then, in May 1965, again at Judith's urging, he recorded almost the same 12 songs – all original compositions – in a professional studio in one hour at a cost of £60. These tracks were released that summer by CBS in the UK as *The Paul Simon Songbook*, and the intensity of his solo performances makes this an essential document of Simon's early years. Alas, it is long since deleted and has never been made available on cassette tape or CD. Six of the songs featured on *Songbook* appear on *Sounds Of Silence*.

Then something rather strange happened. A Boston DJ, perceptively noting that a large proportion of his listeners were thoughtful college students, began playing 'The Sound Of Silence' on a regular basis. The local CBS promotion man heard it on the air and called head office, suggesting it should be released as a single, and Tom Wilson, noting the Byrds-led rise of folk rock, added a rhythm track and electric guitar to Simon & Garfunkel's purely acoustic version. No-one told Paul and Artie, but they found out for themselves soon enough when it became a number one hit. Simon flew home and he and Artie found themselves pop stars. Nothing was ever the same again.

Their second album was recorded in December 1965 during a three-week period at CBS's studios in Nashville and Los Angeles. The speed with which it was made reflects the record company's need to cash in on the sudden success of the single, and was reflected in turn by the rather unimaginative cover shot of Paul and Art glancing backwards, college scarves again intact, as they walked along a dirt track. As it was, it reached only number 21 in the US LP charts but, more importantly, it lingered in the Top Forty for 33 weeks. It remained unreleased in the UK until the Spring of the following year when it reached number 13. As in the US, it stuck around,

eventually spending over two years on the charts.

THE SOUND OF SILENCE

This is the hit single version, with a bass and drum rhythm track and electric guitar added to the vocal track first released on *Wednesday Morning 3AM*. Listen carefully and you can hear variations in tempo necessitated by the studio musicians having to follow the existing track. Although this is the best known version of Simon's first popular hit, the version Simon recorded for *Songbook* is actually superior.

(Students of trivia will probably delight in the confusion over whether the 'Sound' in the title is singular or plural, and whether the title includes the definitive article. It varies according to which album you happen to be looking at. As a general rule, Simon & Garfunkel sang about 'The Sounds Of Silence' while Simon alone sang about 'The Sound...'. The title of this album is most definitely *Sounds Of Silence*, without the definitive article. However, *all* printed sheet music indicates that the correct title of the song is 'The Sound Of Silence', which is how it will be referred to throughout this book.)

LEAVES THAT ARE GREEN

There are many songs dealing with the passage of time in Paul Simon's catalogue. Crossed with unrequited love in the second verse, this the first and probably the prettiest. Backed by intricate guitar picking, the simplicity of the lyrics inspires gentle contemplation but the overall arrangement is in the style of traditional folk music. An untypical failure of imagination may explain the 'Hello/Goodbye' lyrics in the third verse. The notion of Time and its effect on relationships would become a favourite theme for Simon as his own experiences became subtly blended into his work.

BLESSED

Based around the words found in the Sermon on the Mount, what appears to be a reverent song is, in fact, quite the opposite: a despairing, angry text which points an accusing finger at the hypocrisy of the Church. The unusually strident tones of Simon & Garfunkel's voices in unison are enhanced by the dense, almost wall-of-sound-style rhythm track and deliberately paced drum beat on the verses.

As the lyrics indicate, Paul wrote this song after sheltering from the rain in St Anne's Church in Soho. Listening to the sermon in progress, he was struck by the emptiness of the words "It didn't say anything," he said later. "When you walked out of there it didn't make any difference whether you'd walked in. Unless you dug stained glass. Because the meek are inheriting nothing... and that's the basis for this song."

For an alternative view of the Sermon on the Mount, see *Monty Python's Life Of Brian*!

KATHY'S SONG

An uncharacteristically vulnerable love song finds Simon in America, pining for his muse, Kathy, back in England. Before long Simon would approach love songs almost as a disinterested observer, commenting – apparently from bitter experience – on the ups and downs of love from a loftier, intellectual plane, almost as a marriage guidance counsellor might do. Here, however, he opens his heart on a delightful, unselfconscious ballad, using the rain as a metaphor for his loneliness.

SOMEWHERE THEY CAN'T FIND ME

This is an improved re-write of the title track from S&G's début album, telling the tale of a fugitive who's robbed a liquor store and who is anxious to escape retribution. Sung against a harsher backing track, the low-life misery comes across far better than on the original.

ANJI

Davey Graham's slightly bluesy finger-picking guitar instrumental, played with consummate skill by Simon. A very tricky piece too. Simon had befriended Graham on his travels in England. The inclusion of this piece might well have been an altruistic gesture to generate some much-needed royalty money for a guitarist he admired.

HOMEWARD BOUND (LIVE)

The second most enduring song on the album was written by Paul while waiting for a train on Widnes railway station, or so the story goes, and it is as evocative as any road song in the rock'n'roll canon. Not that 'Homeward Bound' is strictly rock'n'roll... it's a wistful, attractive ballad that poignantly laments the loneliness of the long distance singer-songwriter, miles away from home on some god-forgotten railway station, missing his loved ones and yearning for home.

Already released as a single in its studio incarnation – it reached number five in the US charts, and number nine in the UK. This is a live recording but apart from the audience recognition applause after the opening line and some slight adjustments to the vocal inflections, it is almost identical to the studio version. In this respect it served to indicate how precisely S&G could replicate their recorded work on stage – no mean achievement in view of the precision they brought to the studio.

RICHARD CORY

The first of two consecutive songs dealing with suicide describes a scenario in which wealth and fame do not equate with happiness and contentment. In this shrewdly observed socialist fantasy, Richard Cory is a rich playboy, the narrator an employee in his factory who observes his hedonistic lifestyle, apparently with envy, only to discover from a news bulletin that Richard Cory 'went home last night and put a bullet through his head'.

Based on a poem by Edward Arlington Robinson, 'Richard Cory' is sung against a fine upbeat backing track that drives home the story and commended it to others. The best cover version is by Van Morrison and Them, and Denny Laine took a fancy to the song when he was touring with Paul McCartney's Wings in the mid-Seventies.

A MOST PECULIAR MAN

Inspired by a London newspaper item about a loner who committed suicide, 'A Most Peculiar Man' introduced the subject of despair into Simon's catalogue, and at the same time outlined how the inability to communicate that he sang about in 'The Sounds Of Silence' might be resolved in extreme cases.

It was also an early indicator of Simon's tremendous gift for fine detail, with lyrics that suggest how the neighbours might gossip about a suicide on their doorstep. Although it seems that at first S&G are dispassionate observers of this small human drama, their voices grow more strident as the song develops, conveying a righteous sense of shame at the tragedy in their midst.

APRIL COME SHE WILL

Art Garfunkel's showcase on the album, previously sung solo by Simon on *Songbook*, is a delicate love song with a traditional feel, emphasised by lyrics that rely largely on the passing of the months. Again, Simon pits the notion of Time against the duration of an affair, but the simple, attractive melody and velvet smooth guitar picking suggest tenderness and beauty, much like 'Kathy's Song'.

WE'VE GOT A GROOVY THING GOING

"Just for fun," state the sleeve notes describing this throw-away track which was chosen as the B-side to the single of 'The Sound Of Silence', probably because it's an upbeat, rather trivial song which at the very least served to indicate

that the serious young men with their deep spiritual message on the A-side could be as trifling as The Lovin' Spoonful when they were in the mood.

It's lightweight blues/rock in which

the singer pleads for his (or her) lover to stick around because, yes, "We've got a groovy thing going". Funny how words like 'groovy' seem to date so fast...

I AM A ROCK

This sturdy, rather pretentious song comes across almost as a manifesto, and its sentiments seemed to reflect the rather cold, emotionless presence that Simon & Garfunkel radiated when compared to their more fervent contemporaries. With lyrics that seem at odds with the sentiments of other Paul Simon songs of the period, 'I Am Rock' turns Simon's subtle social commentary on its head. If 'The Sound Of Silence' implies that an inability to communicate is at the heart of the nation's ills, here the protagonist seems almost proud of his narrow-minded reclusiveness.

Nevertheless, the insensitive thomo was married to a fine tune, and the song became a number 3 hit single in the US.

Simon and Garfunkel

Parsley, Sage, Rosemary and Thyme

Homeward Bound
The Dangling Conversation
Scarborough Fair/Canticle
Patterns
For Emily, Whenever I May Find Her
The Big Bright Green Pleasure Machine
A Poem on the Underground Wall
Cloudy
A Simple Desultory Philippic (Or How I Was
Robert McNamara'd Into Submission)
The 59th St. Bridge Song (Feelin' Groovy)
Flowers Never Bend With the Rainfall
7 O'Clock News / Silent Night

PARSLEY, SAGE, ROSEMARY AND THYME

ORIGINAL UK RELEASE CBS 62860, NOVEMBER 1966; ORIGINAL US RELEASE COLUMBIA 9363,
NOVEMBER 1966; CURRENT CD: COLUMBIA 032031-2

With more time at their disposal, Simon & Garfunkel went back into CBS's studios to make their third album together, but the success of 'The Sound Of Silence' had kept the duo busy, with the result that Simon had less time to write new material. Because of this, three of the songs on *Parsley, Sage, Rosemary And Thyme* came from as long ago as Simon's period in London and had already been featured, albeit in a more primitive form, on *Songbook*.

Despite the urging of their record company for a quick album to turn over quick profits, S&G spent over three months making *Parsley, Sage...*, mixing it themselves and using an eight-track desk for the first time. In effect, their success enabled them to wrestle artistic control from Columbia, and the fine attention to detail that has been a hallmark of Simon's work ever since starts here.

In 1966 the big three of pop, The Beatles, The Rolling Stones and Bob Dylan, released *Revolver*, *Aftermath* and *Blonde On Blonde* respectively, all of them groundbreaking albums which pushed back the boundaries of popular music, helping to create the much discussed Sixties generation gap in the process. *Parsley, Sage...* did no such thing. Indeed, Simon & Garfunkel presented an image which seemed deliberately designed to bridge that generation gap. Dressed like choirboys on the sleeve and sounding pretty much like choirboys within, S&G were pop stars that appealed to the mums and dads, and it was an image that many potential younger fans might have found difficult to brook. Listen carefully, though, and an element of subversion does emerge, albeit wrapped in far softer packaging than that of their more radical contemporaries.

These considerations made not the slightest difference to the album's commercial success: it sailed up to number 4 in US LP charts and stayed in the Top Forty for over a year. In the UK it failed to chart on release but, given the boost of its successor, *Bookends* and the success of the later single 'Mrs Robinson', it eventually reached number 16 and lingered in the charts for some 66 weeks. A pattern was emerging whereby Simon & Garfunkel's albums did not leap dramatically to the top yet, undramatically, they would seep into the consciousness gradually and sell over a far longer period of time than most of their contemporaries. In the long run, this was very good for business.

SCARBOROUGH FAIR/CANTICLE

This traditional song, re-arranged by Simon and sung to a finely tuned and

rather formal guitar arpeggio, was to become a Simon & Garfunkel favourite. Weaving against the established melody is Garfunkel's anti-war descant, partly derived from an earlier Simon song entitled 'The Side Of A Hill', the full version of which was heard on *Songbook*. Exquisite, note-perfect harmonies freeze the performance in ice.

The song was originally entitled 'Whittington Fair' and there have been suggestions that the credits might have been more honest in denoting the source of the song, specifically that the guitar part was allegedly borrowed from a contemporary arrangement by the British folk singer Martin Carthy. However, there can be no doubt that 'Scarborough Fair' became a Simon & Garfunkel song after this performance.

PATTERNS

Rhythmic bass, bongo drums and a delicately picked acoustic guitar set the mood while Simon, alone and trapped in a routine he finds stifling, reflects som-

brely on how his future will follow a prescribed pattern if, like most, he is unable to control his own life. In the event he had no such problems, but there's a distressing undertone to this song which doesn't benefit from the enhanced arrangement presented here. The starker original, on *Songbook*, is even more disturbing.

CLOUDY

A bouncy, joyous little song in complete contrast to the melancholy sentiments expressed in the previous track and in most of S&G's material of this period, 'Cloudy' suggests balmy California rather than gloomy New York.

'Cloudy' offers a few clues to the composition of Simon's book shelves which evidently contain a breadth of reading matter, from Tolstoy to J.M.Barrie, and the latter's Tinkerbell, Peter Pan's favourite fairy, seems a particularly appropriate character in the context of this song. Light as air and almost a companion piece to '59th Street Bridge Song' below.

BIG BRIGHT GREEN PLEASURE MACHINE

Written in London, apparently while watching his washing tumble around in an all-night laundrette, this is a cynical look at Madison Avenue, and the business of advertising, couched here in the form of a series of unanswered personal questions and a few sly references to sex and the hippie movement. The only way to avoid losing out is to acquire a Big Bright Green Pleasure Machine, whatever that might be. This rolls along at a fast rock pace with an organ predominant in the backing track but the song's strident tones seem out of place amid the more thoughtful songs on this album.

59TH STREET BRIDGE SONG

With its catchy, jaunty rhythm and cheerful lyrics, this song, aka 'Feeling Groovy', was the most obvious hit on the album and it has become universally popular. Flashing repeatedly through four finger-picked chords, its simple rhythm and uncharacteristically cheerful lyrics sug-

gest that New York on a sunny day really is the best place in the world to live.

The 59th Street Bridge links the Upper East Side of Manhattan with the NY district of Queens, clearly a thoroughfare with which Paul and Art were very familiar, though its forbidding iron structure hardly reflects the airy lightness of this song.

It was turned into a minor US hit single by Harpers Bizarre.

THE DANGLING CONVERSATION

After the infectious joy of 'Feeling Groovy', it comes as something of a shock to stumble on another serious song about the inability to communicate, but the sequencing is a deliberate and refreshing contrast. The precise arrangement and thoughtful lyrics about the superficiality of small talk at a time when serious matters need to be addressed make 'The Dangling Conversation' a minor classic, certainly the most sophisticated song that Paul Simon had thus far composed, and certainly the outstanding song on this collection.

It has been suggested (but never confirmed by the inscrutable Simon) that the lyrics of this song are based on T. S. Eliot's poem *The Love Song Of Alfred J. Prufrock*, in which the protagonist is unable to declare his love for fear of offending social convention. Certainly the sentiments are similar, though the thread can be traced back to Simon's familiar theme of suppressed emotions. This time, however, the vehicle for his observations is more sophisticated, the language more literary and, incidentally, the music more mature.

'The Dangling Conversation' was far too refined to succeed as a single, and as a taster for the album it peaked at no 25 in the US charts, never making the listings at all in the UK. Simon was, by all accounts, much disappointed. Perhaps this explains why, in his solo career, Simon never returned to this quality song by re-arranging it to suit the accompanists with whom he would perform live in later years.

FLOWERS NEVER BEND WITH THE RAINFALL

Playing with words – and the truth, if we take the title literally – on a gentle yet fast paced song, Simon twists and turns through a series of inversions – "illusions are real, reality an illusion" – about adolescent confusion and the search for an identity in a confusing world. Another song that first appeared on *Songbook*.

SIMPLE DESULTORY PHILLIPIC

A none too subtle Bob Dylan spoof which if nothing else shows Simon realising that Dylan's work set the standard by which he must measure his own if he was to succeed on a similar level. Vaguely surreal stanzas rhyme in much the same stream-of-consciousness fashion as the seemingly throw-away lines in Dylan's 'Subterranean Homesick Blues', but Simon throws in the names of real characters from the music world, poking fun at music business pretensions and, it seems, having fun himself in the process.

The closing line, "I've lost my harmonica Albert", is a reference to Albert Grossman, Dylan's wily business manager. This track also appears on *Songbook*, albeit in a less realised form.

FOR EMILY WHENEVER I MAY FIND HER

Garfunkel's traditional epic solo performance is a fragmentary, ethereal piece of almost translucent beauty, ideally suited to his choir boy voice, but it's a song which probably makes the later Simon squirm in his sneakers. Brief but haunting, 'Emily' is another of those rare occasions when Simon commits himself to an out-and-out love song without a social observation or a sting in the tail.

Here, on what most critics assume to be a form of homage to the poet Emily Dickinson, he drops all inhibition and lets the arrow fly, holding hands, kissing 'honey' lips and murmuring those three little words while the orchestra heaves like a bosom from the pages of Mills & Boon.

A POEM ON AN UNDERGROUND WALL

Inspired by a real incident on the London tube at Whitechapel, 'A Poem On An Underground Wall', is taken at a fast pace that conveys a restless urgency, the peculiar restlessness of a lone graffiti artist who darts out from behind a dark pillar in the subway to scrawl a four letter word on an advertising poster.

Seemingly fascinated by the role of the loner in society, Simon offers another angle on the alienated fellow, this time conveying the element of fear and the potential for violence that can visit a deserted subway station late at night. This is particularly effective in the fade-out when the final drumbeats chillingly suggest the heartbeat of the writer.

Simon offers no explanation as to why his protagonist feels the need to deface a subway hoarding with obscenities, but the song covers the same ground, and perhaps even the same personality, as the most peculiar man who graced *The Sound Of Silence*.

SEVEN O'CLOCK NEWS/SILENT NIGHT

In which Simon & Garfunkel offer a delicately sung rendition of the famous 'Tannenbaum' Christmas carol while the emotionless voice of a television news reader intones news items about the death of Lenny Bruce, a serial killer in Chicago, race riots in the Southern States and Nixon's desire to accelerate the war in Vietnam despite mounting opposition. "The opposition to the war in Vietnam is the biggest single weapon working against America," Nixon, arch enemy of the counter-culture, is quoted as saying.

The contrast between the beautiful carol with its mellifluous chorus – "Sleep in heavenly peace" and the reality of life in 20th Century America under a crooked President who would later be impeached and sacked for lying, seems all the more profound as each decade passes by. Another poignant exercise in contrasts.

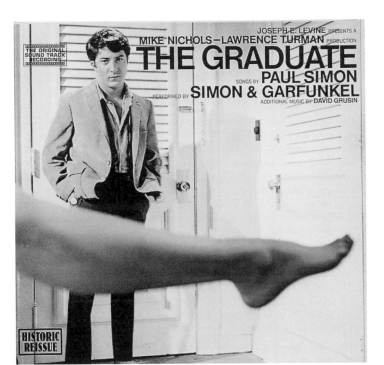

THE GRADUATE

ORIGINAL UK RELEASE, CBS 70042, JUNE 1968; ORIGINAL US RELEASE: COLUMBIA 3180, MARCH 1968; CURRENT CD: COLUMBIA CD 32359

After hearing *Parsley, Sage, Rosemary and Thyme*, film director Mike Nichols invited Paul Simon to compose the soundtrack to his groundbreaking movie *The Graduate.* At first Simon was reluctant but in deference to Nichols' reputation he agreed. In the event, with one notable exception, the soundtrack would comprise previously recorded material, something of a first in movies since until then newly composed music was always used. The album also contains incidental music by Dave Grusin.

The notable exception was 'Mrs Robinson', the song that began life as 'Mrs Roosevelt' and was changed when Simon was informed that Robinson was the name of the film's principal character, played by Anne Bancroft, who sets out to seduce her daughter's teenage boyfriend, a role which established Dustin Hoffman as a formidable acting talent. There are two versions of 'Mrs Robinson' on this soundtrack album, one an instrumental, the other an alternative version to the better known hit single which also appeared on Simon & Garfunkel's *Bookends* LP. In a marketing ploy that now seems inexplicable, both *The Graduate* soundtrack and *Bookends* were released at the same time in the UK and virtually at the same time in America.

'Mrs Robinson' aside, the soundtrack to *The Graduate* includes four previously released S&G tracks and seems therefore to have been something of a marketing exercise that offered little with which S&G fans were not already familiar, unless they were desperate to own the alternative and acoustic version of 'Mrs Robinson' and the incidental film music. Nevertheless, it was a huge commercial success, reaching number one in the LP charts and, like its predecessors, lingering in them for months on end. The film, too, was a huge success, and the combination boosted Simon & Garfunkel's career enormously. Filmgoers not previously familiar with Simon & Garfunkel's music heard their dulcet tones wrapped around 'The Sound Of Silence', 'Scarborough Fair' and 'April Come She Will', and bought the album in droves, probably unaware that the same songs were available, together with many others, on two earlier albums. Chances are they discovered this fact later and bought the other two albums as well. It's therefore quite likely that the soundtrack to *The Graduate* is one of the most bought, yet least played, albums in history.

Full track listing: 'The Sound Of Silence', 'The Singleman's Party Foxtrot'*, 'Mrs Robinson' (instrumental), 'Sunporch Cha-Cha'*, 'Scarborough Fair/Canticle', 'On The Strip'*, 'April Come She Will', 'The Folks'*, 'The Great Effort'*, 'Big Bright Green Pleasure Machine', 'Whew'*, 'Mrs Robinson', 'The Sound Of Silence'. (*Indicates incidental, non-Simon & Garfunkel material.)

BOOKENDS/SIMON & GARFUNKEL

BOOKENDS

ORIGINAL UK ISSUE: CBS 63101, JUNE 1968; ORIGINAL US ISSUE: COLUMBIA 9529, JUNE 1968; CURRENT CD: COLUMBIA CD 63101

Paul Simon & Art Garfunkel were an odd couple, mismatched physically and emotionally, but their voices could produce the most gorgeous synthesis. Garfunkel was tall and gangling, with a shock of curly blonde hair that seemed impervious to the attentions of a comb, and a personality that seemed both overtly romantic yet skittishly whimsical. Simon was short and stocky with flat, straight hair, of serious demeanour and ostensibly unyielding in his concentration and intensity. Garfunkel was light and airy, Simon dark and brooding.

All the best qualities of these two strangely disparate characters coalesced now on *Bookends*, the first vinyl side of which was the most cohesive series of songs they ever recorded together. Unfortunately Simon went through a period of writer's block in the months while it was being made, which left side two of the vinyl edition somewhat bereft of new material and less cohesive, even if it did contain their biggest hit single since 'The Sound Of Silence'.

What was side one in the days of vinyl is programmed deliberately to offer a conceptual theme, a snapshot of a day in the life of America in the Sixties as it might be seen from several different age groups. And it has to be said that Simon's view of his country is relentlessly critical, with random violence, political disillusionment, marital discontent and a failure of society to care for its old, all tearing America apart. Not that the pessimism of his views makes for bad music: with one exception, Side One of *Bookends* is a remarkable piece of work which sounds as fresh in the Nineties as it did when it was recorded. Side two, however, consists largely of tracks that had been previously released as seemingly unconnected singles, though its stand-out track, 'Mrs Robinson', would become one of the most popular songs of the era.

The idea of offering a concept, or at least a cycle of related songs designed to follow in sequence, was quite new in pop music in 1968, and it was a bold move, as was the fuller production on many of the songs. While in the past S&G had relied largely on Simon's guitar and occasional orchestration for accompaniment, on several songs on *Bookends* they threw in all manner of extras, crowding the track almost to the point of saturation. 'Save The Life Of My Child', 'Fakin' It', 'Hazy Shade Of Winter' and their concurrent single, 'Mrs Robinson', all indicate that Simon, at least, was not prepared to stick to the tried and tested, acoustic guitar led, formula that had brought them so much success. Garfunkel, on the other hand, seemed more likely to want to rest on his laurels – as his future solo career would indicate.

Bookends followed *The Graduate* soundtrack to the top of the American charts and, like its predecessors, lin-

gered in the upper reaches for several months. It also made number one in the UK where its success rejuvenated the S&G back catalogue, sending *Parsley, Sage, Rosemary And Thyme* into the charts 18 months after its original release.

BOOKENDS

A brief instrumental preface introduces, on acoustic guitar, the *Bookends* theme which will surface later on the album.

SAVE THE LIFE OF MY CHILD

With a plethora of studio effects, the album proper opens with an acutely observed piece about the craziness in American society. A slash of synthesiser and a fuzz bass add to the madhouse mood, while phased background vocals imitate the terrifying screams of bystanders at an urban calamity, in this case a suicide leap from a New York skyscraper. Deep down in the mix Garfunkel can be heard singing the opening line of 'Sound Of Silence', suggesting that the teenager's impending suicide is motivated by his inability to communicate. On another level, of course, the screams come from a terrified society sliding into an abyss of its own making.

The key line here is "What's become of our children?", a common inquiry from an older generation raised in the ultra conservative Thirties, Forties and Fifties who looked on askance while American teenagers defied the draft, took drugs, rioted on their campuses and worshipped rock and roll stars.

AMERICA

'America' is without doubt the most impressive song on *Bookends*, an exquisitely produced ballad with a gorgeous descending signature on the verses and an uplifting chorus of anthem-like proportions. Part narrative, part fragmentary, all blank verse, its literal interpretation is of a journey across America that Simon and his partner Kathy undertook as tourists, discovering the country and each other, but on a broader, allegorical sweep it suggests that all of America's restless children are simultaneously embarking on the same journey, to discover themselves and their role in America's changing society.

Simon's attention to detail is scrupulously observed here, from the cigarettes and magazines to Mrs Wagner's pies and the man in the bow-tie, but the central theme is best expressed in the key line "I'm empty and aching and I don't know why", a reflection of the sense of disillusionment that Simon's generation felt about the way their country was being governed, and the way those in authority required them to live their lives.

Although never released as a single, 'America' would become one of Paul Simon's best known and best loved songs. Like 'The Sound Of Silence', he would return to it in concert, generally as an encore, for two decades.

OVERS

First, curiously, there's the scratch of a match striking, a cigarette or perhaps even a joint being inhaled, followed by a diminished chord, then Simon sings wistfully about the end of a relationship. Here, the unusually simple, stark accompaniment is surely designed to reflect the emptiness of a relationship that has become a habit – like saccharin, as Simon tartly observes. Garfunkel joins in mid-way through to give the song a rounder tone but even his warmth cannot disguise the coolness that has beset this particular couple. Time, another favourite topic, seems to drag here. The alliance is a waste of time but neither party seems able to take the initiative and end it once and for all.

This song was rejected for inclusion in *The Graduate*, though it might well have been written about the stale relationship between Mrs Robinson and her husband.

VOICES OF OLD PEOPLE

Not a song but, quite literally, the voices of sad and occasionally angry old people resigned to a dreary life waiting to die. This was Garfunkel's contribution to the *Bookends* concept of growing old, but it's a low spot in a diet of otherwise remarkable music. The actual voices were recorded in California, at two old people's separate homes.

OLD FRIENDS

Finally, at the conclusion of side one in the vinyl edition, we find two old men seated, on a park bench, both of them turned 70, with nothing but memories to prop them up. Jimmy Haskell's string arrangement adds poignancy to the gentle pace as melancholia dominates the fade-out, a coda that returns to the *Bookends* theme which opened the album and which further echoes the theme of memories. Our two old men are not relishing their lot, and the sense of pathos is almost overwhelming as the song, and side one of the vinyl release, draws to a close.

Aging is a subject not often touched on in popular songs, especially those aimed at a young audience, but here it's treated with great respect. Indeed, not until John Prine wrote and recorded the moving and much covered 'Hello In There' in 1971 would age be treated with such dignity in a pop song.

FAKIN' IT

This is a re-arrangement of an earlier version of the same song which was released as a single in August 1967. This time around the tempo is speeded up, while the fat production suggests a sense of claustrophobia, even desperation. Lyrically, the song explores the feeling of inadequacy, while the central section offers Simon's reflection on his previous life, or at the least the life of an ancestor, as a Central European Jewish tailor.

The song is also notable for the curious ringing of a shop bell and the Englishwoman's voice inquiring whether "Mr Leitch" has had a busy day. It was the voice of folk singer Beverly Martyn, who happened to be friendly with Donovan, then Britain's answer to Dylan. Donovan's surname was Leitch.

(The B-side of this single, 'You Don't Know Where Your Interest Lies', never appeared on any S&G album and is otherwise unavailable today. A rather slight song, its non-PC lyrics – implying "you'd be a fool to leave me" – would probably raise an outcry today.)

PUNKY'S DILEMMA

Paul Simon has always been attracted to surrealism and 'Punky's Dilemma', quite the oddest piece on this collection is his first stab at converting such images into a lyric, in this case a light, gentle paced song. "I wish I was a Kellog's cornflake, floating round in my bowl takin' movies," he sings, somewhat whimsically. After two verses of apparently innocuous allusions to breakfast, Roger the draft dodger is introduced, along with a mild-anti-war theme. Finally, someone – presumably Roger – can be heard falling down a flight of steps.

MRS ROBINSON

Mrs Robinson, Anne Bancroft's role in *The Graduate*, and 'Mrs Robinson', the energetic hit single that saw Simon & Garfunkel top the US charts for four weeks in April 1968, bear little resemblance to one another on the surface – though there is an air of suppressed frustration in its lyrics that just might have catapulted her into the arms of Benjamin, the Dustin Hoffman character twenty years her junior.

Either way, the song began life not as a paean to Anne Bancroft's character but with the title 'Mrs Roosevelt' which, with three syllables, scans equally well. Then Mike Nichols, the film's producer, butted in. "I was sitting around writing it but I was singing 'Mrs Roosevelt'," Simon told Bill Flanagan. "I was singing 'Mrs Robinson' too. Art said to Mike Nichols, 'Paul's writing a song called "Mrs Robinson".' He said, 'You're writing a song called "Mrs Robinson" and you didn't tell me?' I said 'Well I don't know whether it's "Mrs Robinson" or "Mrs Roosevelt".' He said, 'Don't be ridiculous. We're making a movie here, It's "Mrs Robinson"'."

The song is carried along by Simon's urgent, choppy rhythm guitar and full-throated vocals which coalesce around images that suggest the heroine is trapped in a life of petty pleasantries, the stifling conservatism in which the American middle-classes floundered before they came to terms with their free-thinking sons and daughters as the Sixties came of age. In this respect, 'Mrs Robinson' would have been thematically appropriate to have been included on side one of *Bookends*.

'Mrs Robinson' has other intriguing moments. The name Jesus appears in the choruses, the first time it had been used in a song, and certain radio stations refused to play it as a result. In a move as cowardly as it was senseless, Frank Sinatra covered the song and changed the name 'Jesus' to 'Jilly'. Finally, the third verse suggests that one reason why America is losing its way is because the country no longer has idols to look up to, wholesome idols like the baseball star Joe Di Maggio. (Simon probably chose Joe Di Maggio because he required a five syllable name to scan correctly but, in the light of the song's subject matter, it is interesting to note that Di Maggio was the husband of Marilyn Monroe and was thus, mythically if not technically, cuckolded by the Kennedys, whose era was ending as Simon wrote this song.)

There have been other cover versions of 'Mrs Robinson' besides the puerile Sinatra effort, most notably The Lemonheads who turned the song into an unlikely punk thrash in 1992.

HAZY SHADE OF WINTER

This was an old song, written back during Simon's stay in England, and its inclusion here was doubtless due to the paucity of new material on hand, especially as Simon has since expressed dis-

satisfaction with it. Only the driest hint of optimism is detectable in a song about the aging process, as observed through the changing seasons. Don't give up, he seems to be saying amid choppy orchestration which grates unsympathetically with the melancholy overtones.

A lively, top-heavy cover version by The Bangles reached number one in the US in 1988, and number three in the UK the same year.

AT THE ZOO

In the Seventies Paul Simon would become a regular guest on the satirical TV show Saturday Night Live, and as a paid-up member of the lively New York Jewish intellectual circle, he was certainly drawn to satire as an outlet for criticism and creativity. Here, amusingly, and in a song whose lively pace and light arrangement seems at odds with the lyrical content, he depicts society as a series of stereotypes, all of whom remain in their separate cages, like the unfortunate animals in Central Park Zoo.

Simon is adept at cushioning a harsh lyrical message in music that suggests otherwise, and in this respect his major influence may have been Randy Newman, the widely admired West Coast Jewish singer-songwriter whose cynical view of America was almost always couched in the sweetest of tones.

Simon
and
Garfunkel
Bridge
Over
Troubled
Water

BRIDGE OVER TROUBLED WATER

ORIGINAL UK ISSUE: CBS 63699, FEBRUARY 1970; ORIGINAL US ISSUE: COLUMBIA 9914
FEBRUARY 1970; CURRENT CD: COLUMBIA 462488-2

Simon & Garfunkel went out in style with this blockbuster album, a multi-million seller which at the time set sales records and, if they weren't already, turned the duo into household names. As their career progressed, S&G took longer and longer to complete their work in the studio, and with the exception of two hastily contrived tracks, the lengthy gestation period of this album marks another important landmark in Simon's eternal search for perfection.

It also marked the end of the partnership. Paul and Artie weren't getting along any more: Paul wanted absolute control over the way his songs sounded, and Art wanted to be a film star. Work on the album was held up while Garfunkel filmed his scenes in *Catch 22*, which annoyed Simon. He was also annoyed, not to say insulted, when the hierarchy at CBS pleaded with him not to go it alone, suggesting that without Garfunkel he was unlikely to succeed. The record company's attitude, of course, was further intensified by the extraordinary sales figures the album notched up.

In many ways the *Bridge Over Troubled Water* album became an icon of its era, its dull blue-grey cover and washed out picture of Simon & Garfunkel suggesting the doom and gloom that must surely follow the end of the 20th Century's most colourful decade. So many homes had a copy of this album that its songs became as well known as classics by The Beatles, but two and a half decades later it's difficult to justify exactly why it became the seller that it did. There were two huge hit singles, of course, in the title track and 'The Boxer', but at least four of the songs, all of them up-tempo efforts, were inferior by the standards that Simon had set himself on earlier albums, and because of this there's a slightly patchy feel to *Bridge Over Troubled Water* that wasn't present on *Bookends* or even *Parsley, Sage, Rosemary and Thyme* for that matter.

Perhaps it was *because* they split up that Simon & Garfunkel's final album attracted buyers in droves, all of them greedy for a final slice of the most successful duo of the Sixties now that the decade was over. Perhaps it was because the two singles were so good, as good as anything that S&G ever recorded, that buyers assumed the whole album must be chockfull of wonderful tracks. Or perhaps it was because the record industry as a whole was approaching a boom period and Columbia (CBS in the UK), under the guidance of the dynamic Clive Davis, was leading the way.

Bridge topped both the US and UK charts in February 1972. In the US it remained on the charts for 24 weeks but in the UK it stayed on the charts for an extraordinary 303 weeks.

BRIDGE OVER TROUBLED WATER

This elegant, majestic, piano-led ballad, the effective climax to Simon & Garfunkel's partnership, has now become a popular standard, the most covered song that Simon ever wrote. Epic in its sweeping grandeur, 'Bridge' glides through three verses at a stately pace, evoking images of the power of healing followed by a transcendent conclusion to life's burdensome journey. The resonant piano is played by session man Larry Knechtel.

Art Garfunkel's reading of the song has a hymn-like quality, which suggests the gospel influence that Simon would bring out on later live versions after S&G split up. But Garfunkel's mellifluous tenor is a far cry from the heaving gospel interpretations that Simon performed with The Dixie Hummingbirds and which, he often stated, was his preferred reading of the song. Garfunkel, of course, felt differently and wasn't afraid to say so.

There have been over 50 cover versions of 'Bridge Over Troubled Water' by such disparate artists as Elvis Presley, The Jackson 5, Perry Como, Lena Martell and Willie Nelson, not to mention a slew of male voice choirs. As a single, S&G's version topped the charts in both the US and UK in February and March of 1970.

serene, somewhat deliberate pace established by the fretted instruments of the South American group, Los Incas, whom Simon had apparently first encountered and befriended in Paris many years ago. The melody is borrowed from a Peruvian folk song and Simon adds his own lyrics, subtitled 'If I Could', which offer a common sense, albeit somewhat prosaic, philosophy about life's choices.

EL CONDOR PASA

Although not nearly so well known as the stately title track, in retrospect 'El Condor Pasa' can be seen as the most important track on the whole album. More than any other song in the Simon & Garfunkel catalogue, it pointed to the direction that Simon's music would take for the next twenty years, insofar as it indicated his growing interest in music from regions other than North America (and Europe).

In its own way, 'El Condor Pasa' is also a stately anthem, flowing at the

CECILIA

A light-hearted, up-tempo romp dominated by the percussive track over which Simon sings, probably fairly spontaneously, about a faithless ladyfriend who invites another man into her bed while the singer is in the bathroom! The track was conceived in Los Angeles, at a house Paul and Artie rented in Beverly Hills, while the duo experimented with the reverb on Art's tape machine. Joined by Paul's brother Eddie on guitar, they created the backing track there and then. Other instruments – and the vocals – were added later in the studio.

By Simon's standards, 'Cecilia' sounds like a throwaway, an experimental dance track with a carefree, sing-along vocal, but it comes as a refreshing change after the stately pace of the title track and the rather po-faced lyrics of 'El Condor Pasa'.

Recently, it was covered without distinction by Suggs, the singer from Madness.

KEEP THE CUSTOMER SATISFIED

Maintaining the brisk pace, this is an update on 'Homeward Bound' but instead of longing to return to his love life, our troubadour is now quite simply fed up with the road, dead tired and longing for some peace and quiet. Some might argue that singing about the displeasures of rock stardom, and the boredom of being on the road, smacks of sour grapes when you've banked a million dollars and, off the road, enjoy a lifestyle akin to an emperor, but there

can be no doubt that Simon, at least, was tired of Simon & Garfunkel, though not necessarily of his career in music. Not one of the most distinguished offerings on *Bridge*.

SO LONG, FRANK LLOYD WRIGHT

Sung by Garfunkel alone, this lush ballad operates on two levels, firstly as a tribute to the celebrated American architect, and secondly as a nostalgic look back to the S&G partnership as it comes to an end. It also acts as a tribute from Simon to his buddy who might have become an architect had Simon's songs not got in the way.

With a melody that comes close to the stateliness of the title track, the lyrics suggest the parting round the corner and is one of two instances on the album where Simon drops his guard slightly, and admits to having second thoughts about ditching a partner who could sing as beautifully as Art. In the long fade-out Paul and producer Roy Halee can be heard faintly, chanting: "So long, already, Artie". Keep raising the volume and a logical conclusion can be heard just before the track fades to silence.

THE BOXER

Staking its claim to stand alongside the very best songs Paul Simon has ever written, 'The Boxer' is a subtle commentary on man's inhumanity to man and, more crucially, a scathing castigation of American society's preoccupation with winners and lack of tolerance for losers. It's also a fine tune, propelled by a fast, intricate quitar figure that underpins the melody, lingering and returning over ebbs and flows from major to minor chords until the song breaks out into its swaggering, full-throated climax. It's quite possible, too, that 'The Boxer' was the first song to incorporate the word 'whore' in its lyrics and, by extension, on to the US airwaves.

The possible identity of the 'boxer' has been the subject of some speculation. Some have suggested it is about Bob Dylan, who covered the song on his *Self Portrait* album in 1970, while another school of thought thinks it is about Simon himself, though the details of the boxer's life are clearly not autobiographical. However, a song doesn't have to be literally true or about a specific individual. The hero of the song is the archetypal underdog hero, standing up bloody but unbowed to all that society (or even rock critics) can throw at him.

Unlike so many of the songs from the Simon & Garfunkel era, 'The Boxer' refuses to date, and Simon has repeatedly returned to the song in concert over the years, often changing the arrangement and, on many occasions, adding a central verse not heard in this original version which suggests that time cannot erode the value of anything that is genuinely virtuous. Such sentiments – and the line "After changes upon changes we are more or less the same" – inevitably win heartfelt applause from long-time fans.

As a single 'The Boxer' reached number seven in the US charts, and number six in the UK.

BABY DRIVER

It's to be hoped that Simon's point of view was tongue-in-cheek on this rocker with apparently smug, self-satisfied lyrics about his well-to-do family, comfortable lifestyle and, in the final verses, determination to experiment sexually.

As seems to be the pattern on this album, the up-tempo songs carry considerably less weight than the slower songs into which far more thought and care has been invested. Like 'Keep The Customer Satisfied' and 'Why Don't You Write Me', which follows, 'Baby Driver' is quite dispensable, and it is the inclusion of these inferior tracks that always begs the question as to why the album as a whole sold as remarkably as it did.

ONLY LIVING BOY IN NEW YORK

Unusually, Paul takes the lead vocals on a slow, dramatic ballad which in different circumstances might have been more suited to Garfunkel's style and voice. As the lyrics imply, however, Simon wrote

this touching song while Art was away in Mexico filming *Catch 22* – looking for a future without his old friend Paul – and, like 'So Long, Frank Lloyd Wright', there's more than a suggestion of regret in Simon's words. Tom, of course, refers to Tom Graph, Jerry's partner in the Tom & Jerry days of long ago.

The song is carried by another beautiful melody, well up to the standard of the title track and the other outstanding ballads on this record.

Everything But The Girl's eloquent cover of this song scraped into the UK Top 50 in 1993.

WHY DON'T YOU WRITE ME

Simon's first stab at reggae is unconvincing. He would later admit as much and, to make amends, travel down to Jamaica to record the infinitely superior 'Mother And Child Reunion' on the next album he made. With slight lyrics that castigate a poor correspondent, the rhythm track is amateurish and clumsy, a poor imitation of the real thing, and a further example of the yawning gap between the quality songs on *Bridge* and the largely uptempo throwaway stuff.

BYE BYE LOVE

Until the emergence of S&G, The Everly Brothers were the most successful duo in American popular music and it seems fitting that their successors should offer some sort of tribute as they retired from the contest. 'Bye Bye Love' was Don and Phil Everly's début hit in 1957, a sorry tale of lost love set to the kind of rhythm that suggests it doesn't really matter because we're all young and we'll fall in love with somebody else next week anyway.

Simon & Garfunkel's version, recorded live during the previous year, stays faithful to The Everly Brothers' arrangement, and is executed with appropriate finesse and gusto.

SONG FOR THE ASKING

This charming closing ballad is a plaintive declaration of love, touching in its simplicity, brief but heartfelt. Take me as I am, imperfections too, Simon is saying in this particularly honest declaration of modesty.

Significantly, the closing song on the final Simon & Garfunkel album features Paul solo, though ballads like this, and the three that precede it here, would be few and far between in his solo career. Without Art to sing them, Paul Simon seemed far less inclined towards the smooth, harmonious ballads that grace this album. A pity.

PAUL SIMON
THE PAUL SIMON SONGBOOK

CBS 62579   AUGUST 1965

For reasons best known to himself, Paul Simon has chosen not to allow any record company to re-issue his earliest solo work which he recorded for CBS in 1965 during his second protracted stay in London. This is a great shame, for these original versions of many of his earliest songs are performed with a passion that is somehow lacking on the better known versions that he recorded with Art Garfunkel. All serious artists are constantly moving forward, leaving behind their past without much regret, and Simon is no exception as his later career shows. His enthusiasm for this material would decline over the next twelve months, as his rather downbeat sleeve notes indicated, and this probably explains why the version of these songs that appear on Simon & Garfunkel's first three albums appear somewhat clinical in comparison.

It was not uncommon in the mid-Sixties for sleeve notes to be written by artists themselves and, perhaps influenced by the manner in which Bob Dylan wrote surreal notes on the back of several albums during this period, Simon warms up with a surreal dialogue of his own before explaining his motivation behind the album: "This LP contains twelve of the songs that I have written over the past two years. There are some here that I would not write today. I don't believe in them as I once did. I have included them because they played an important role in the transition. It is discomfiting, almost painful, to look back over something someone else created and realise that someone else was you. I'm not ashamed of where I've been and what I've thought. It's just not me anymore. It is perfectly clear to me that the songs I write today will not be mine tomorrow. I don't regret the loss."

In addition to Simon's own summing-up of the material, his friend Judith Piepe offered her own rather fanciful analyses of the material, with the exception of one song 'He Was My Brother' about which Art Garfunkel wrote: "I first heard this song in June 1963, a week after Paul wrote it. Cast in the Bob Dylan mould of the time there was no subtlety in the song, no sophistication in the lyric; rather, the innocent voice of an uncomfortable youth. The ending is joyously optimistic. I was happy to feel the way the song made me feel. It was clearly the product of a considerable talent."

It is an indication of how prolific Simon was during his early years that these songs, as recorded by Simon & Garfunkel, are spread out over their first *three* albums. The songs were recorded in a studio in London's Bond Street in barely an hour at a cost of just £60. Simon, who received an advance of £90 for the work, is accompanied only by his own acoustic guitar, and only one microphone was deemed necessary. Although

Reginald Warburton and Stanley West are credited as producers, the production is minimal. Having sung them every night for weeks, Paul was very familiar with the songs he elected to record and only one take was required. The simple sleeve featured Paul seated on a cobbled street alongside Kathy, his London girlfriend.

One track from *The Paul Simon Songbook*, 'Leaves That Are Green', appears on Simon's box set, *Paul Simon 1964-93*.

[Do not confuse this album with a widely available compilation album of cover versions of Paul Simon songs by various artists, also titled *The Paul Simon Songbook* (Connoisseurs Collection VSOPCD 173, released June 1992).]

Full track listing: 'I Am A Rock', 'Leaves That Are Green', 'A Church Is Burning', 'April Come She Will', 'The Sound Of Silence', 'A Most Peculiar Man', 'He Was My Brother', 'Kathy's Song', 'The Side Of A Hill', 'A Simple Desultory Phillipic', 'Flowers Never Bend With The Rainfall', 'Patterns'.

PAUL SIMON

CBS 69007/WARNER BROS 25588 FEBRUARY 1972

Free at last of the obligation to indulge Art Garfunkel with songs arranged with high vocal harmonies or provide his former partner with an opportunity for a grand solo performance, Simon naturally turned to his interest in reggae, Latin American rhythms and blues for his first solo outing, which as a result became a showcase for his talent at working in virtually any musical style you care to name. It also changed the emphasis from the lyrics, usually the dominant element on Simon & Garfunkel records, to the music.

Characteristically, Simon took his time over his first solo project and, wisely, it was very much a low key affair compared to the final S&G album. It was recorded variously in Jamaica, Paris, New York, Los Angeles and San Francisco, and it exuded a more downbeat, less formal atmosphere than the records he'd made with Art Garfunkel. Conscious that his solo work would be compared with what had gone before and that *Bridge Over Troubled Water* was still selling by the bucketload two years after release, Simon switched gear, had more fun musically and wrote lyrics that seemed more personal, and more downbeat, than ever before.

Whether they really were more personal is open to conjecture for the inscrutable Simon was never one to bare his soul too openly and, as ever, lyrical enigmas were a crucial part of his style.

Reviewing the album in *Rolling Stone* magazine, the erudite Jon Landau drew attention to Simon's propensity for marrying sombre lyrics to a cheerful tune, and was favourably impressed: "Simon's music, rather than abounding in blatant and obvious attempts at expressing the soul, serves as a continually ironic counterpoint to the emotions, ideas, images and feelings expressed in the lyrics." It was, said Landau, Simon's most personal and painful work thus far... "this from a lyricist who has never shied away from pain as a subject or theme."

After the enormous success of *Bridge Over Troubled Water*, Paul Simon's first solo album was destined to become a noble failure in sales terms, but its chart performance nevertheless augured well for his future as a solo performer. It reached number four in the US charts but stayed around for only 18 weeks. In the UK, it reached no 1 and stayed in the charts for 26 weeks.

MOTHER AND CHILD REUNION

The title of Simon's second and far more successful stab at reggae came, believe it or not, from the name of a chicken and egg dish he saw on the menu in a Chinese restaurant.

Set against a remorselessly catchy tune and an infectious beat of which Bob Marley himself would surely have approved, the song is about renewing a relationship after death. It was inspired by the death of Paul's pet dog which had

been run over by a car, which brought on thoughts of his own family's mortality. "It has nothing to do with my mother," he told interviewers. "What I'm talking about here is the unbelievable, shattering experience of death."

The lively reggae feel might seem inappropriate to this profound subject, but contrasts such as these were becoming increasingly common in Simon's work. Recorded at Dynamic Sound Studios in Kingston, Jamaica, it features a group of local reggae musicians who by all accounts were much bemused by the time and trouble Simon took over the recording. Usually, they knocked off tracks in a couple of takes – several a day, in fact, and were paid $10 a track. Simon took a week over one track, which necessitated negotiating an altogether different pay structure!

DUNCAN

Simon has always denied that his songs derive directly from personal experience, and it's unlikely that Duncan's adven-

tures on his road from the Maritimes bear the slightest trace of Simon's own background. But from the sincerity of his tone, and the detail he brings to Duncan's story, he makes it sound as if he is singing from bitter experience.

This is Simon at his narrative best, a chirpy melody with a fast insistent rhythm pushing things along while he recounts a tale in which the attention to detail is paramount, especially in the emphasis on Duncan's awakening sexuality. Lines such as "The couple in the next room, bound to win a prize, they've been going at it all night long" and "She said 'Here comes something and it feels so good', just like a dog I was befriended" add a touch of slightly ribald humour to a subject not often covered as frankly as Simon does here.

The accompaniment is by Los Incas, the South American group who played on 'El Condor Pasa' on *Bridge...* and who would accompany Paul on some of the material he would perform on his first solo tour.

EVERYTHING PUT TOGETHER FALLS APART

Though some critics interpreted this title as a metaphor for the Simon & Garfunkel split, this is Simon's fairly overt warning about the dangers of drug taking, the personality changes that uppers and downers can bring and, finally, the messy business of overdosing. Like needles stuck into veins, it's unsentimental, far from glamorous and, appropriately, it is locked into a melancholy blues tempo.

Simon later stated that his main reason for writing the song was not to alert his fans to dangers of dope but merely to include the word 'paraphernalia' in a pop song!

RUN THAT BODY DOWN

Hot on the heels of his drug alert, Simon further advises his fans to opt out of the rat race, not to overstretch themselves and take a break from time to time. Evidently, this advice came from his own doctor. Simon had recently given up smoking both cigarettes and the occasional grass joint.

The deliberate beat sits behind a melody that sounds as it if has been derived from chamber music, but overall the song lacks inspiration and is one of the album's weaker tracks.

ARMISTICE DAY

This was an old song, begun in 1968, which Simon felt was inappropriate for Simon & Garfunkel, and it was written in a D tuning he no longer favoured. An unremarkable tune is wedded to lyrics concerned with the desperation of the peace movement.

"Let's have a truce. I just meant that I'm worn out from all this fighting, from all the abuse that people are giving each other and creating for each other," Simon told Jon Landau. "It's not a protest song. Protest songs are a little trite at the moment," he told *New Yorker* magazine.

ME AND JULIO DOWN BY THE SCHOOLYARD

Whatever the lyrics might be implying on this upbeat, quite startling track, the mood is set by the furiously strummed, Calypso styled rhythm guitar which echoes the music preferred in Corona, an area of Queens which is largely inhabited by Puerto Ricans.

Simon, as narrator, is an immigrant, bragging about his exploits – teenage naughtiness one suspects – though the specifics are left unclear. "Something sexual is what I imagine, but I never bothered to figure out what it was," Simon said later. "Didn't make any difference to me." There were even suggestions, from no less an authority than the author Truman Capote, that it was about homosexuality but Simon has always denied this.

A terrific rhythm, a catchy melody and chord work on a par with Pete Townshend, but as a single 'Me And Julio...' reached only no 15 in the UK and no 22 in the US.

PEACE LIKE A RIVER

This sombre song about turbulence and unrest bemoans lost idealism, and the disillusionment of the Sixties idealists, and is perhaps a precursor for the more substantial images contained in the far superior 'American Tune' on Simon's next record.

The strange deep noises in the central section were by all accounts created by playing the low notes on a piano, halving the speed and playing the tape backwards.

PAPA HOBO

A relaxed song about a subject that is anything but unrelaxing – urban pollution. The city in question is probably Detroit, the centre of America's automobile industry. Carbon monoxide is referred to as 'perfume'. "What I'm really talking about there is the fact that cars give us our freedom at the same time they're killing us with carbon monoxide," Paul told interviewers who asked him about this bluesy piece.

HOBO BLUES

A relaxed blues instrumental featuring the celebrated French jazz violinist Stephane Grappelli.

PARANOIA BLUES

This rather disturbing song about urban violence was inspired by being searched at US customs. "Every time I fly into JFK from Europe, they take me into this little room, lean me up against a wall and search me for drugs, presumably because I have long hair and I'm carrying a guitar," Simon revealed. " The first time it happened I was scared stiff."

Evidently paranoid about street violence, Simon sympathies with those who are worried about being victims of crime. The bottleneck guitar is played by Stefan Grossman.

CONGRATULATIONS

Larry Knechtel's smooth electric piano sets the mood for a gentle, sophisticated song about the break-up of marriage which in tone and tempo acts as a precursor to the type of jazz-tinged work that Simon would eventually offer on his 1975 album *Still Crazy After All These Years*. There's more than a touch of cynicism in offering congratulations to a divorcing couple, and as he ponders over the fragility of relationships, Simon's world-weary lyrics seem to suggest that divorce is practically inevitable in modern day America.

In choosing to end his first solo outing on such a pessimistic note, Simon reinforced the dark, depressing tone of the record as a whole. He would lighten up as the decade progressed.

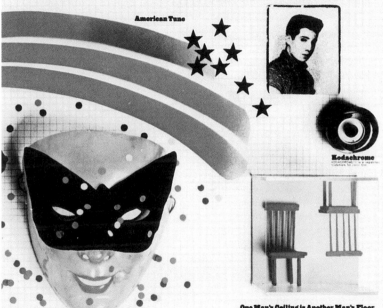

Paul Simon

There Goes Rhymin' Simon

American Tune

Kodachrome

KODACHROME is a registered
trademark for color film

Take Me to the Mardi Gras

One Man's Ceiling is Another Man's Floor

THERE GOES RHYMIN' SIMON

CBS 69035/WARNER BROS 25589 MAY 1973

Encouraged by the relative success of his first 'proper' solo album, Simon went back into the studio almost immediately and, within 18 months, a second solo effort hit the shops. By his standards this was quick work indeed.

There Goes Rhymin' Simon had a far lighter touch than his previous record, and this was reflected in the cover on which the songs were represented by quirky images, including an eye for 'Kodachrome', a leg in plaster for 'Learn How To Fall' and a chair stuck to a ceiling for 'Another Man's Floor'. The lyrics were less pessimistic, the rhythms more joyous, the atmosphere more carefree. With this album, Simon seemed to be deliberately trying to shake off the serious image which had clung to him for so long.

Most of the album was recorded in Muscle Shoals, Alabama, where the local studio had won a reputation for its funky qualities and the skill of its regular session crew, including guitarists Jimmy Johnson and Pete Carr, bassist David Hood, drummer Roger Hawkins and keyboard player Barry Beckett, all of whom appeared on most of the album's songs.

In the US charts *There Goes Rhymin' Simon* reached number two and stayed on the charts for 24 weeks. In the UK it made number four and stuck around for 22 weeks.

KODACHROME

"When I look back to all the *crap* I learned in high school," must have been a satisfying line to sing, and as the opening line on the album it seemed to indicate that Paul Simon was now his own man, and would not be dictated to. Naturally America's radio stations took

THERE GOES RHYMIN' SIMON: PAUL SIMON

offence at the line but that didn't stop 'Kodachrome', the first single to be taken from the album, from reaching number 2 in the *Billboard* Hot 100. Kodak, the photographic materials giant, also took offence, not to the lyrics but to the use of their trademark. Wisely, in view of its promotional potential they chose not to injunct the song but to Simon's chagrin they insisted that a small © was added next to the song's title on the sleeve and elsewhere.

It's a bright, catchy song, a perfect album opener, which rattles along at a cracking rock'n'roll pace. The breezy lyrics, ostensibly about photography, contain typical Simon references to colours and weather, and the nostalgia that photo albums can bring.

TENDERNESS

Slowing down the tempo, Paul tackles a simple ballad with doo-wop overtones, with velvet smooth backing vocals from The Dixie Hummingbirds and an evocative horn arrangement by Alan Toussaint.

With lyrics exploring the difficulty in maintaining a balance in relationships, 'Tenderness' is neatly sequenced to offer a satisfying contrast between the fast paced opener and the joyousness of...

TAKE ME TO THE MARDI GRAS

The loping rhythm of this charming song reflects traditional New Orleans styles, especially those associated with the famous annual bacchanalian festival, and its sleepy feel echoes the lazy character of this, the most charming of US cities. Enlivened by the fine counterpoint falsetto voice of the Rev Claude Jeter, and delayed echo guitar from Jimmy Johnson, there's a lovely, but all too brief, Dixieland jazz fade-out from the Onward Brass Band to emphasise the location.

By all accounts Claude Jeter, a man of very high moral principles, insisted on hearing lyrics to the entire album, lest some contain profanities, before con-

senting to take part. Perhaps he overlooked the 'crap' that Paul learned at
high school!

As a single, 'Mardi Gras' reached
number 7 in the UK in April 1972.

SOMETHING SO RIGHT

One of Paul Simon's loveliest melodies
wraps itself around a song about his
eternally confused emotional state and
man's difficulty in expressing himself.
The sweeping strings were arranged by
Quincy Jones.

ONE MAN'S CEILING IS
ANOTHER MAN'S FLOOR

Opening, and closing, with an eerie
descending riff, this is a rare Paul Simon
blues excursion, led by Barry Beckett's
honky-tonk piano. The song is about
paranoia, one of Simon's favourite subjects, and living in ignorance of the habits
of one's neighbours.

AMERICAN TUNE

This may have been a deliberate shot at upstaging 'Bridge', and it certainly came close. The undoubted highlight of the album, 'American Tune' is Simon's attempt to make sense of US history, from the arrival of the Pilgrim Fathers to the impeachment of Richard Nixon and, like 'Bridge', is epic in construction, beautifully phrased, and hymn-like in its beauty and vision. Written at the time when America had been shamed by Nixon and the Watergate scandal, it is nevertheless optimistic, patriotic even, its stirring final verse suggesting that dented national pride and uncertainty can withstand underhand politics, that the image of the Statue Of Liberty will offer succour, just as it did to the thousands of European immigrants who gazed up at it as they arrived in America for the first time.

The stately tune was borrowed from Bach's Sacred Heart of St Matthew, and Simon's lyrics, especially those lines about the Mayflower, seem entirely appropriate. A genuine masterpiece, and

Rolling Stone magazine's Song Of The Year in 1973.

WAS A SUNNY DAY

From the grandeur of 'American Tune' to a lively, hypnotic but largely inconsequential beach calypso celebrating the balmy weather of the Gulf of Mexico. Charming but unimportant, almost an update of '59th Street Bridge Song', the backing vocals are by Maggie and Terre Roche of The Roches.

LEARN HOW TO FALL

Perhaps inspired by watching his toddler son fall over several times a day, Simon offers sound advice in one of the album's lesser songs, depicted on the sleeve by a foot in a plaster cast! Bright and breezy, the kind of the song that might have appeared on a Simon & Garfunkel album a decade earlier, it features a piping organ in the background.

ST JUDY'S COMET

Any weary parent who's ever tried to lull his young child into sleep at the end of a tiring day will sympathise with this gentle, attractive lullaby. "If I can't sing my baby to sleep, well it makes your famous daddy look so dumb," sings Simon, gently mocking the contrast between his public persona and the reality of his private life. It is rare that Simon writes such a genuinely autobiographical song.

"I don't think it ever helped him to fall asleep," Simon admitted. "Babies don't fall asleep to lullabies. They fall asleep when they're ready to fall asleep. There's no real St Judy's Comet, I took the title from the drummer for Clifton Chenier whose name was Robert St Judy."

There are no drums on this track, just an ambient sound of percussion leaking into the studio microphones. In 1975 Simon played the song on *Sesame Street*, the long-running children's TV show.

LOVES ME LIKE A ROCK

The album closes with a joyous slab of gospel music, arranged in the call and response style of America's Southern preachers in the Forties and owing just about everything to the singing of The Dixie Hummingbirds.

Love not being a characteristic of rocks (!), it can be assumed that the rock in question is a religious reference. A rousing climax to an album in which Simon further extended his range of musical styles, though they would be filed away for the immediate future, only to reappear in far more dramatic form almost a decade and a half later.

Paul Simon · Still crazy after all these years.

STILL CRAZY AFTER ALL THESE YEARS

CBS 86001/WARNER BROS 25591 OCTOBER 1975

The most difficult achievement for maturing popular singers during the second half of the Seventies was to retain the audience they had attracted during the Sixties. It was a shrinking audience that had less time to listen to pop music and less money to spend on it, as the 'kids' became parents themselves. With the additional indignity of insolent young punks and new wavers dismissing them as dinosaurs and 'old farts', the lesser artists from the Sixties simply retreated behind closed doors, stuck their heads in the sand, and delivered more of the same to a dwindling audience with diminishing returns, or, even worse, retired to the golden oldie cabaret circuit. The better equipped sought to develop their work to match the changing tastes of their audience.

A songwriter as intelligent as Paul Simon naturally chose the latter, and on this recording he introduced a more sophisticated jazz sound into his music while at the same time emphasising the delicacy of his lyrics and, as ever, wrapping up the whole package in pristine, state-of-the-art production. For the time being, he dropped the stylistic variety of the music on his previous two recordings in order to accentuate the theme of sad nostalgia for times and lovers past, a subject that his maturing audience might readily appreciate as they left their twenties behind them.

The result was his most mature sounding record yet, as far removed from the folk-singer of old as, in time, *Graceland*, would be from this collection. His public agreed, sending *Still Crazy After All These Years* to number one in the US on release, albeit for one week only. In the UK it reached only number 11.

An additional achievement of this album, and its title track, was to add a now commonly used phrase to the English language.

STILL CRAZY AFTER ALL THESE YEARS

Every so often Paul Simon will write a line which finds an instant rapport among his audience, in this case the opening shot, "I met my old lover on the street last night". Glancing backwards to acknowledge the passing years with a feeling of regret must surely have been a common experience for many of those thirty-somethings who bought this album. Correctly sensing that his maturing audience would identify with these emotions, Simon went further, hinting that when an enjoyable evening of nostalgia is over, when friends have departed, loneliness creeps in with the inevitability of the advancing years. Even on a piece as gentle as this, there's a suggestion of bitterness. Every generation feels the same: things ain't what they used to be.

Barry Beckett's electric piano is the principal instrument, gliding serenely through the gorgeous melody, while Mike Brecker's alto saxophone solo introduces the jazz element that informs so many of the songs that follow. The effect of the song is to announce to his audience that Paul Simon has grown up.

The old lover, of course, was assumed by some to have been an oblique reference to Artie who turned up on the next song...

MY LITTLE TOWN

Continuing the theme of nostalgia, this song marked the reunion of Simon & Garfunkel and, in an amicable (if not consumer friendly) gesture, the track appeared on Garfunkel's concurrent *Breakaway* album as well as *Still Crazy*. Indeed, both albums were released on the same day.

'My Little Town' opens as a gentle autobiographical piece looking back towards childhood, carrying schoolbooks, mum doing the laundry, saluting the flag, but as the song develops there is an echo of something altogether more sinister: the feeling of frustration, and the desperate urge to escape which is the soundtrack of the small-town ambience.

It is a boring, unchanging, unvarying place, lacking imagination, freedom and individuality. In the dull dead of night, the town's sons are twitching, and trigger fingers too. As the menace increases, so the backing track rises up and shuts out the S&G harmonies, and a cacophony results.

Take away those aching harmonies, substitute a hoarse vocal and tighten the flowing rhythm track and you'd have one of Bruce Springsteen's dark parables, the kind of the song that might have appeared on his *Nebraska* album eight years later.

It was Simon's intention to offer Art something darker than the mellifluous ballads that had graced his previous solo albums. With 'My Little Town' he succeeded admirably. "I thought it was time for him to sing a really nasty, biting lyric," Simon told NY writer Bill Flanagan. "That song was entirely an act of imagination, as opposed to autobiography. There's no element of me in it there at all," he added.

I DO IT FOR YOUR LOVE

The third song in the opening trilogy of nostalgic reminiscence finds Simon looking back over a failed affair and, as ever, excelling in the tiny details. Taken at a gentle pace which never falters, 'I Do It For Your Love' appears to be an out-and-out love song until the final verse when, as ever, love sadly fades, like the rug he bought in the junk shop.

50 WAYS TO LEAVE YOUR LOVER

With its catchy chorus, apparently taken from a series of rhymes written to amuse his young son, '50 Ways To Leave Your Lover' became Paul Simon's first American No 1 hit since 'Bridge Over Troubled Water'.

Opening with Steve Gadd's deliberately paced march drum beat, the verses stick to a simple, attractive melody which ticks over into a series of practical, if hokey, not to mention callous, suggestions on how to conclude an affair. On the verses Simon appears almost to be talking, as opposed to singing, yet he switches gear on the faster choruses.

NIGHT GAME

After music, baseball is Paul Simon's great love and it was natural that sooner or later he would bring the sport into a song. The funereally paced 'Night Game' deals with the close of an unsuccessful season and the simultaneous death of the squad's old pitcher. As ever, it's the small details that enhance the song – the losing scoreline, the ritualistic elements of the pitcher's last rites, how his spikes are laid on the pitcher's mound. Toots Thielman's harmonica adds an appropriate touch of melancholia to a wistful melody.

GONE AT LAST

This fast paced gospel song was originally intended as a duet with Bette Midler but in the event it was Phoebe Snow who turned in a fine performance, trading lines with Simon over rollicking

piano and the Jessy Dixon Singers. They're hoping that a long streak of bad luck has finally gone and judging from the joyous atmosphere they conjure up, especially on Ms Snow's high pitched fade out, good fortune is just around the corner.

SOME FOLKS LIVES ROLL EASY

A gentle paced plea to the Lord for help in times of need, this song floats by in the smooth, easy-going style that Simon has made his own. The first verse contrasts the different ways in which lives can evolve, while the second sees the singer knocking on the pearly gates, seeking succour even though he "ain't got no business here". Finally, there's the realisation that most folks lives don't roll easy at all.

HAVE A GOOD TIME

A lazy, relaxed tempo sees Simon throwing off his troubles in uncharacteristically whimsical fashion, laughing in the face of disaster and even recommending a good dose of hedonism as an antidote to ageing. "God Bless The USA", sings Simon, somewhat tongue-in-cheek, suggesting that blind patriotism is just as likely to take the country to the brink of disaster as anything else. The mood is smooth and joyous, and only Phil Woods' closing sax solo jars the senses.

YOU'RE KIND

Yet again Simon chooses to cushion a song about broken romance in the softest of settings. Cool, restrained and catchy, 'You're Kind' deals with the idiosyncrasies of love, how one partner might be blissfully unaware that the other is on the point of ending the relationship. "... (it's) a sort of a cruel song," Simon told Bill Flanagan. "It's an indifferent song. Someone treats you real nice and you say 'I'm leaving'. You could say it's for an arbitrary reason: 'I like to sleep with the window open and you sleep with the window closed'. Or you could say it was about freedom. It works either way... (and) that makes it a better song. There are people who can't stand to be locked in and there are people who don't give a damn and simply decide, 'It's better for me so I'm leaving'."

SILENT EYES

Somewhat strangely, Simon chose to close 'Still Crazy' with a rather cold and unmelodious song which appears to be a re-affirmation of his faith in God, a curious enigma since Simon has often spoken of his indifference to religion. Dramatic, almost psalm-like insofar as it lacks anything that might be described as a catchy chorus, 'Silent Eyes' sees Simon again knocking at the pearly gates, along with the massed voices of the Chicago Community Choir. "'Silent Eyes' is about the Jews but it wasn't about religion," Simon has said. It's a sombre, rather anti-climactic way to close this otherwise warm toned album.

ONE TRICK PONY

WARNER K 56846/WARNER BROS 3472 AUGUST 1980

Pop stars have yearned to be film stars ever since Elvis appeared in *Love Me Tender* way back in 1956, and Paul Simon, although no-one's idea of a romantic leading man, was no exception. His acting experience may have been limited to a walk-on part in *Annie Hall,* and a few very funny cameo appearances on *Saturday Night Live,* the hilarious cult comedy show produced by his friend Lorne Michaels, but that didn't seem to daunt him, and it has to be said that his realistic performance as Jonah, a struggling and ageing singer-song-writer, in *One Trick Pony,* was far better than most would have suspected.

Simon's character, Jonah, was a one-hit wonder whose career after the hit has been a series of disappointments. He brought to the role a resigned and unsentimental weariness that reflected with no little accuracy the underside of rock's glittery front. Unfortunately, and unfairly, the film bombed, perhaps because Jonah's existence simply wasn't glamorous enough to attract a wide audience. It was never released in the UK and has only ever been shown on TV once. It is not available on video. Similarly, the soundtrack recording was a rather low-key, unexciting album, its songs constrained by hav-ing to fit into the plot of the movie.

One Trick Pony marked a shift in record labels, from Columbia Records to Warner Bros, largely because the latter agreed to finance this movie. It was a blow for Columbia to lose an artist of the magnitude of Simon and in time the rights to his solo catalogue would trans-fer to the new company. (Simon & Garfunkel recordings remain on Columbia, or CBS in the UK, however.)

That blow was not immediately apparent, as the soundtrack to *One Trick Pony* was a commercial disappointment and Simon's worst selling album in years. Indeed, the shift in labels coincided with a decline in Simon's market success that would not be arrested until *Graceland* six years later. *One Trick Pony* attained only twelfth place in the *Billboard* listings and slipped off the charts far quicker than his earlier albums. In the UK it made only number 17.

The best known song – indeed, the only truly memorable song – from *One Trick Pony* is 'Late In the Evening', the opening cut, which slides along at a brisk, rockabilly tempo, hastened by the terrific, Mexican styled stabs of brass, Steve Gadd's perpetual drums and a fine bass riff. Written after Paul and his band had been jamming around the 'Mystery Train' riff played by Elvis, Scotty Moore and Bill Black in 1955, ensemble playing as good as this would, as the song suggests, almost certainly 'blow that room away'.

"The horn part was written by Dave Grusin," Simon would later explain. "It's as famous as the song. And I thought it was a great horn part... It always sounded like a kind of mariachi thing in the middle of a track that had a 'Mystery Train' groove to it. When I first heard it I said, 'It's great but it's not what the song's supposed to be'. But it was so great that I said, 'I guess it is what the song is going to be'."

'That's Why God Made The Movies' is shuffle paced, and takes its inspiration from the François Truffaut film *L'Enfant Savage*. Littered with obtuse Freudian imagery, linking lovers with mothers and sex with childhood, there's a warm chorus and nice slide solo from Hugh McCracken.

The title track, 'One Trick Pony' is a slow shuffling rocker featuring an outstanding solo from Eric Gale on guitar. The lyrics dwell on Jonah's limitations as an entertainer. Audience applause is dubbed on at the end to suggest a live recording.

'How The Heart Approaches What It Yearns', the most memorable song on the album after 'Late In the Evening', is a gentle song with an odd time signature which sees Jonah musing poignantly on his yearning for success. At less than three minutes, it is regrettably short. The lovely nylon string solo is played by Eric Gale. "It's a wonderful solo," Simon has said. "(And) It has a very evocative lyric. To me, the lyric on this song does feel like it fits the character of Jonah Levin. But the 10.8 time signature probably doesn't. The Belvedere Hotel in the opening was the A&R Recording studio on 48th Street in NY."

'Oh Marion' is rather bland by Simon's standards, with a slow, light jazzy feel. The slightly discordant flugelhorn adds a curious touch.

At almost six minutes 'Ace In The Hole' is the longest song on the album and a journey through time signatures. Opening with a hot rhythm with slapped bass, Simon duets with keyboard player Richard Tee, before the song reverts to a rock steady pace with plenty of soloing before the funk returns.

'Nobody' is a slow love song taken at a gentle pace with lyrics that are almost spoken. There's a pleasant, floating electric guitar solo from Eric Gale, and the multi-tracking on Simon's voice gives a rich choral effect.

'Jonah', as the title suggests, is an autobiographical piece about the central character in *One Trick Pony* with Simon's evocative attention to detail in his descriptions of Jonah's pre-show ritual. 'God Bless The Absentee' has a catchy piano riff and its central portion seems like a re-write of 'Homeward Bound'. Finally, 'Long Long Day' returns to the theme of weariness, one of Simon's favourite subjects. "Don't see my face in *Rolling Stone*," sings Jonah after 24 years on the road, once more lamenting his lack of success.

PAULSIMON

HEARTS AND BONES

HEARTS AND BONES

WARNER BROS 923942-1, NOVEMBER 1983

Reunited with Garfunkel for a concert in New York's Central Park on September 19, 1981, Simon bowed to public demand and continued the reunion, though no-one was ever under the illusion that it would be permanent. The following year Simon & Garfunkel toured Europe and America together, offering a selection of their greatest hits as well as some of Simon's better known solo songs. They also made plans to record together again, much to the delight of their fans and record label, but behind the scenes all was not well – the two old friends couldn't see eye to eye on the type of songs Simon wanted to record and, in the end, it was rumoured that Simon wiped Garfunkel's vocal tracks from the recordings that to a large extent made up *Hearts And Bones*.

Whatever the background to *Hearts And Bones*, there is a school of thought among Simon devotees that this album is an overlooked masterpiece. Unfortunately, it arrived at a time when Simon's commercial stock was at his lowest, and it sold poorly, but in its songs Paul Simon lays bare his soul as never before. Perhaps it was the personal nature of the songs that alienated Art, or the fact that Simon seemed for once to have deliberately eschewed his professionalism and tin-pan alley craftsmanship in favour of emotion. Either way,

it seemed that Simon no longer cared whether he had a hit or not, or even what the critics might say. This was *his* album, the album *he* wanted to make. After twenty-five years in the business, he was certainly entitled to it.

There was much to admire on *Hearts And Bones*, and if any criticism could be levelled towards the album, it was that it lacked the stylistic unity from which *Still Crazy After All These Years* had benefited. But although the styles of music chopped and changed, there *was* a continuity in the theme of those songs

– about half the album – which dwelt on the undulating course that relationships can take. By this time in his life Simon had encountered the ups and downs of romantic fortune on more than a few occasions, and it was inevitable that these experiences would sooner or later find their way into his music. 'Hearts And Bones', both versions of 'Think Too Much', 'Train In The Distance', 'Cars Are Cars' and to a lesser extent 'When Numbers Get Serious' all deal with shifting emotions – "the arc of a love affair", as Simon ingeniously characterises the subject in the album's title track.

In general the critics were kind to the album, perhaps because it wasn't quite so obviously commercial as Simon's previous offerings, and most pop critics tend to pour scorn on blatant hit material. It was greeted with rave reviews on both sides of the Atlantic, but reviews – good or bad – have never made that much difference when it comes to shifting units. With no concurrent hit singles to raise Simon's profile *Hearts And Bones*, like the *One Trick Pony* soundtrack, was

another commercial failure, especially by Simon's previous standards. Indeed, it fared even worse than *One Trick Pony*, reaching only a disappointing no 34 in the UK and 35 in the US.

ALLERGIES

This wry comment on America's obsession with allergies had its basis in fact. Around this time Simon was suffering from calcium deposits on his fingers which made it painful, if not impossible, to play guitar. He brought in his brother Eddie, who ran a Guitar School in New York, to deputise for him on one tour – hence the lines "My hands can't touch a guitar string, my fingers just burn and ache", but thankfully the problem abated.

Opening the album at a cracking tempo, 'Allergies' is enlivened by Al Di Meola's outstanding electric guitar solo, certainly the fastest, trickiest playing ever to grace a Simon track.

'Allergies' became the album's first single, backed with 'Think Too Much', but it failed to chart, as did the album's other two singles 'Hearts And Bones' and 'When Numbers Get Serious'.

HEARTS AND BONES

'The Late Great Johnny Ace' aside, 'Hearts And Bones, the title track, is the key song on this album and, at five and half minutes, one of the longest pieces in Simon's entire catalogue. Ebbing and flowing over a lovely, cascading melody, it's clearly an autobiographical song about lost love with clear references to Simon's failed relationship with the actress Carrie Fisher, best known for her role as Princess Leia in *Star Wars*. "One and one half wandering Jews" is clearly Simon's description of himself and Fisher, whose father, the singer Eddie Fisher, was Jewish, and there can be little doubt either about the meaning of the line, "returning to their natural coasts" – he to the East, she to the West.

"That's one of my best songs," wrote Simon in the notes that accompanied his 1991 box set. "I was beginning to understand about writing... how to do it, when to use ordinary language and when to use enriched language. The line 'the arc of a love affair' is really what the song is about."

Airto Moriera's percussion propels the song along, and the climax is neatly sequenced to link directly into...

WHEN NUMBERS GET SERIOUS

... a far less serious song, initially about the social niceties of exchanging phone numbers. Fast paced, quirky and deftly played, this song sees Simon playing with number/word associations, developing the theme of exchanging telephone numbers and its attendant perils – "Please don't give it to some madman," he sings – into more complex numerical equations.

THINK TOO MUCH (B)

Not often does the same song appear twice on one album in different tempos, but it does here. Simon had spent many hours in therapy and the experience clearly affected his muse as well as his understanding of his own mind. After recording a fast paced version of 'Think Too Much' – 'Version A' – Simon decided he'd treated the subject too lightly and went back to record this more thoughtful version.

Clearly inspired by his relationship with Carrie Fisher, it comments on how different sides of the brain control our capacity for intellect and emotion, and how one can be dominated by the other... if we allow it to by thinking too much. The identity of the "smartest people in Los Angeles" remains a mystery; perhaps they're Paul's analysts, perhaps they're the Hollywood press, who found much to write about, as ever, when two celebrities become an item.

SONG ABOUT THE MOON

At a time when Simon was recovering from another spell of writer's block, he offers a tongue-in-cheek primer on the art of songwriting. "If you want to write a song about the moon, if you want to write a spiritual tune, then do it," he advises, suggesting that the only way to overcome writer's block is to drag the song out with brute strength.

During the Seventies Paul's guitarist brother Eddie's New York musicians' workshop, The Guitar Studies Center, held classes for aspiring songwriters as well as guitarists, and from time to time Paul visited the school to give the pop equivalent of a 'master class'. 'Song About The Moon' might even have been the basis for one of his lectures.

THINK TOO MUCH (A)

This fast paced, original version of 'Think Too Much' omits the flowing introduction in version B and gets straight to the point – the vicissitudes of the cranium – before musing on the imprudence of trying to mould another person into the object of one's dreams. Though the quicker tempo renders this version nowhere near as cerebral as Version B, the sentiments are, in fact, just as profound as those of anyone who's tried to remodel someone else must surely have discovered. The lighter feel is emphasised by Steve Ferrone's insistent drums, emphasised by rhythmic hand claps.

TRAIN IN THE DISTANCE

Again, Simon opens up his heart in what appears to be a song about his first marriage. The opening lines refer implicitly to his first wife Peggy, who was married at the time they met, and who came from America's South, but as the song develops the perspectives become less specific as Simon muses yet again on failed romance. Anyone who's ever heard the sound of an *American* train hooting in the distance, especially on an otherwise silent night, well knows how it carries a romantic, mournful aura that acts as a perfect metaphor for broken romance.

Married to one of Simon's lovely flowing melodies, the metaphor is all the more striking.

As ever Simon was coy about the autobiographical details. "That was a very personal song it's true," he said. "Maybe (it's) literally true, maybe it isn't. What's the difference? The story isn't really what's important, the point of it is. Therefore I said: 'So I'll tell my exact story'. So what? It doesn't make any difference. So, in a way, even though it was entirely personal, I depersonalised it by saying, 'What's the difference what the story is? It could be my story. It could be yours. It doesn't matter'."

RENEE AND GEORGETTE MAGRITTE WITH THEIR DOG AFTER THE WAR

The song with the longest title in Paul Simon's entire catalogue is an appropriately surreal, unusual and quite remarkable piece of songwriting, inspired by the caption to a photograph of the French painter and his wife that Paul saw in a book. Dreamy, descriptive verses about Magritte and his wife's day out shopping in downtown New York give way to a chorus that name checks a string of do-wop vocal groups, The Orioles, The Penguins, The Moonglows, The Five Satins, all of whose records Simon listened to as a teenager.

There is a sparkling consonance to the lyrics: "easily losing their evening clothes", "brought tears to their immigrant eyes", "in the cabinet cold of their hearts", and the way in which the verses flow effortlessly into the chorus belies Simon's consummate craftsmanship.

Although it's not been performed live, there is plenty of evidence to suppose that 'Renée...' is one of Paul Simon's personal favourites. "It holds together on a level of surrealist imagery as a Magritte painting would, because I juxtapose two things that wouldn't normally be in the same frame: the Magritte couple and the R&B groups of the Fifties," he told Bill Flanagan in a lengthy analysis of this song in Flanagan's book *Written In My Soul*. "That song has a

mood about it that seems to be right... it makes me feel something specifically."

CARS ARE CARS

This fast paced, initially somewhat edgy, song makes the shrewd observation that while cars all over the world are pretty much the same, people can be annoyingly different. The contrast is emphasised by a nice change in tempo, as the urgency of the motorised verse gives way to an easy paced, flowing melody over which Simon contemplates how people "change with the curve". Re-assuringly, lest we're left with the impression that he prefers cars to people, Simon resolves his dilemma by observing that his life would have been far less interesting if those with whom he'd shared it had the characteristics of a car!

Midway through, there's an arresting bit of stereo separation which on first hearing is nothing less than freakish. Without warning, Simon's quite deep speaking voice states 'Drive 'em on the

left' in the left hand channel/speaker, followed by 'drive 'em on the right ' in the right channel/speaker. These spoken words are recorded so sharply that the unwary are seriously likely to believe that someone else is in the room with them, at least on first hearing.

THE LATE GREAT JOHNNY ACE

Simon's heartfelt tribute to John Lennon stands well apart from the album's theme of shifting emotions, yet for many it is the stand-out track on *Hearts And Bones* and is among the most poignant songs that Paul Simon has ever composed. Drawing a parallel between the headstrong Beatle and Johnny Ace, the Texas rocker who died while playing Russian Roulette back in 1954, it also recalls Simon's own past, the period he spent in England during "the year of The Beatles, the year of the Stones". The verses were written long before the bridge, which Simon wrote only after Lennon was so senselessly murdered. In less careful hands, a Lennon tribute might come across as either mawkish or overtly reverential, but Simon strikes a perfect balance here, recalling Lennon and his golden era with subtlety and restraint. Instead of attempting to heap praise on Lennon's enormous contribution to 20th Century music, Simon conveys the moment of Lennon's death with a stark recollection of how he spent that particular evening after he heard the news. Most other bars probably rang out with the sound of Johnny's music that night too.

The haunting orchestral coda, arranged by Philip Glass, effectively evokes Lennon's mid-period, the acid – tinged backwards effects of 'Strawberry Fields Forever' and his *Revolver* and *Magical Mystery Tour* songs.

PAUL · SIMON
GRACELAND

GRACELAND

WARNER BROS 925447-2, SEPTEMBER 1986

In the summer of 1984, as he faced the problem of furthering a critically successful but commercially waning career, Simon received a gift from his friend Heidi Berg which set him on the road towards what many critics believe to be his masterpiece. The gift was a bootleg tape from the townships of South Africa called *Gumboots: Accordion Jive Hits No 2*, and it changed his musical direction radically.

He spent the rest of the year seeking out similar black African music and, thoroughly inspired by his researches, went to South Africa in February 1985 to spend 17 days recording with local musicians in Johannesburg's Ovation Studio.

Graceland, however, was not recorded solely in South Africa, nor did it consist only of South African music, nor was its subject matter African-oriented. The album was recorded in New York, Los Angeles, London and Louisiana as well as Johannesburg, and included tracks with Cajun and Hispanic backing musicians. While South African mbaqanga and mbube rhythms dominate the music, adding a unique flavour which up to this point was largely unknown in America and Europe, the songs actually fuse South African elements with American pop, thus rendering the unknown more palatable to ears already tuned to Paul Simon. The majority of the tracks were backed by musicians from the townships, and the experience of writing for and in such a different musical tradition was an obviously liberating experience. While the concerns about which Simon chose to write are those of an American writer – and he is too honest a writer to wish or be able to renounce *his* cultural heritage – his open response to other cultural heritages loosened the bounds of his songwriting and seems to have enabled him to find a new language, both musically and lyrically.

The release of *Graceland* was met with as much political criticism as artistic acclaim. In 1986, South Africa was still ruled by the minority National Party régime, and the essentially peaceful "velvet revolution" (to borrow a description more usually applied to Eastern Europe) which followed from the release of Nelson Mandela, and Prime Minister De Klerk's recognition that Apartheid was no longer sustainable, was some years away. Sanctions still applied, and a major focus of the anti-Apartheid movement was on high profile sporting and cultural events. Although the principal purpose of the boycott as it affected musicians was to prevent middle-of-the-road or pension-seeking rock dinosaurs cashing in at the notorious white playground of Sun City, Simon had clearly broken the letter of the sanctions regulations. *Graceland* thus attracted more controversy than Paul Simon, eternally quiet, diligent and uncontroversial, had attracted in his entire career.

In vain did Simon plead that, far from offering succour to the oppressor, he had been popularising (and paying well) some of the very "victims" the sanctions were intended to benefit. He had wandered into a political minefield. To those who argued that any breach of sanctions was unacceptable – and this position is understandable both in theory and as a propaganda weapon – any counter-argument based on artistic grounds was irrelevant. In the final analysis, however, the artistic merits of *Graceland* figure more substantially in the history books than the fierce contemporary denunciations that were, in the event, soon overtaken by events.

The album was a massive commercial success, especially in the UK where, after reaching No 1, it lingered in the charts for almost two years. In America, where radio stations are traditionally less attuned to styles of music that don't comply with their rigid formatting process, *Graceland* reached no 3, though it stayed in the Top 200 for 97 weeks, eventually selling four million copies.

_____

THE BOY IN THE BUBBLE

The growl of accordion with which the album begins states immediately that this is a *different* Simon product. With a nod to the *Gumboots* bootleg which had sparked his first interest in South African music, Simon lets his musical co-writer, the accordionist Forere Motloheloa, signpost the direction the album will take. It is a direction which, in its dense, churning rhythms, owes little or nothing to the blues, to Chuck Berry, or to the American folk and tin pan alley traditions in which Simon had made his reputation.

The subject matter – the horrors and insubstantiality which underpins the "days of miracle and wonder" – is less of a radical departure from Simon's previous work, but he brings a vividness to the lyrics (the juxtaposition of "the bomb in the baby carriage", for example), as well as a "serious playfulness" (witness the alliteration of "the boy in the bubble and the baby with the baboon heart"), which clearly shows the extent to which new music had irrigated his imagination. His lyrics add an ironic counterpoint to the upbeat, cheerful swing of the music, but it is not his purpose merely to moan about the awfulness of life on "a distant constellation that's dying in a corner of the sky". He is more knowledgeable, more compassionate and more of a poet than that. (And if you doubt the poetic qualities of the song, try achieving in other words the same concise effects as Simon does in the final lines - "these are the days of miracle and wonder, and don't cry, baby, don't cry".

"'The Boy In The Bubble' devolved down to hope and dread," Simon told *Rolling Stone*'s David Fricke. "That's the way I see the world, a balance between the two, but coming down on the side of hope."

'The Boy in the Bubble' was released as a single in the UK, where it reached no 26 with the help of a stunning video which, in 3D, placed Simon in the jungle, surrounded one minute by wild animals and the next by state-of-the-art technology.

GRACELAND

Joy and sorrow; history and today; America and Africa – in the album's title track Simon brews a medley of contrasting ingredients into a song as fine as any he has written. The bubbling, insistent, sinuous playing of Baghiti Khumalo on fretless bass and Ray Phiri on guitar provides a perfect counterpoint to the American music which the song celebrates – the Mississippi Delta, home of the blues and memorably defined as "shining like a National guitar"; Elvis Presley, whose Graceland home is the object of the singer's pilgrimage; and The Everly Brothers, early influences who repay the compliment with their backing vocals on the fade out.

But the song is no mere trip down nostalgia lane. Simon's concerns, and those of the "poorboys and Pilgrims with families" who share his journey, are contemporary. The singer is not only divorced ("the child of my first marriage" accompanies him) but also a recent loser in the game of love (the bittersweet phrase "she comes back to tell

me she's gone" tells of a fresh, unhealed wound). Nor is his sympathy reserved for his own misfortunes. His "travelling companions are ghost and empty sockets"; he empathises with the "girl in New York City who calls herself the human trampoline".

The jaunty music, with its traces of rockabilly, might seem callous and insensitive set against the lyrics, with their clear-eyed view of the emotional detritus of modern life, and such a contrast is just the sort of thing Simon excelled at earlier in his career. Simon's purpose, however, is not to express pity – either for himself or for the other casualties "bouncing into Graceland". The happy accident of Presley's choice of name for his famous and magnificent abode allows Simon to play with the religious notion of redemptive grace. Though not previously, nor here, a religious writer, Simon presents music itself as offering a form of salvation. "Maybe I've a reason to believe we all will be received in Graceland," he concludes.

Bob Dylan expresses a similar belief

in the redemptive power of music in "Mr Tambourine Man", and curious to observe that, though written at a much earlier stage of his career, it too, like 'Graceland', reflected a distinct change of style from the writer's previous work.

I KNOW WHAT I KNOW

This collaboration with General M.D. Shirinda and The Gaza Singers is a lighter piece, contrasting the Shangaan voices of South Africa with febrile chatter of the New York party scene. The song itself stands as a tribute to Simon's self-confidence in his new work. He can afford to quote the party-girl's put downs ("she thought I was alright ... in a sort of a limited way for an off-night" and "there's something about you that really reminds me of money") as well as his own feeble chat-up line ("aren't you the woman who was recently given a Fulbright"). The repeated line "don't I know you from the cinematographer's party", brilliant in its scansion and rhythm, neatly encapsulates the empty socialising of the New York arts crowd.

Simon, while clearly not averse to *attending* such parties, is not the prisoner of that scene, and has no illusions about the permanence of fame and reputation. He is, at this stage of his life and career, his own man. "I know what I know, I'll sing what I said, we come and we go, that's a thing that I keep in the back of my head."

GUMBOOTS

As the title indicates, this song is another tribute to the accordion-based music that had triggered his initial interest in the sound of Soweto. Backed this time by The Boyoyo Boys, Simon tackles a subject perennially popular with poets and song-smiths – love. Among the challenges which this subject presents is the difficulty of finding anything new to say but Simon rises to this challenge. Three vignettes which show different ways of failing to communicate are separated by a chorus which elegantly sums up a feeling every lover has suffered at one time or another. "You don't feel you could love me but I feel you could". The song ends with a repeat of the opening two lines, as if to make the point that this is a process that goes around and around forever.

This was the first song that Simon heard on his bootleg tape. It is the style of music favoured by mine and railroad workers in SA; 'Gumboots' are the heavy boots they wear at work.

DIAMONDS ON THE SOLES OF HER SHOES

Unlike the previous songs on the album, which were initially recorded in Johannesburg, 'Diamonds...' was recorded entirely at the Hit Factory in New York, when Ladysmith Black Mambazo were in town for an appearance on *Saturday Night Live*. Curiously, the song opens, unlike the "African" songs, with a verse in Zulu. It also features the popular West African star Youssou N'dour, as well as our old friends Baghiti Khumalo and Ray Phiri.

Ladysmith Black Mambazo open the song a cappella, before the familiar bouncing beat kicks in and establishes a cheerful, danceable groove driven headlong by the startling bass guitar of Baghiti Khumalo. The lyrics themselves are somewhat obscure. The rich girl whose non-standard footwear provides the title seems to be involved both with the singer, who takes her for granted, and, doubtless on the rebound, with a poor boy whose "ordinary shoes" can only walk her to a doorway on Upper Broadway.

Maybe there are metaphors here, or subtle allusions to New York street life, or a surreal re-working of the 'Down in the Boondocks' theme. Maybe Simon is just having fun – "and I could say 'oo oo oo ...' as if everybody knows what I'm talking about".

YOU CAN CALL ME AL

Rumour has it that this song has its origins at a party Simon hosted during which he met the composer Pierre Boulez for the first time. As he was leaving, Boulez called Simon 'Al' and the hostess, his then wife Peggy, 'Betty'.

Whether or not this is true, the song itself has moved a long way from such a simple social misunderstanding. Its theme is an old Simon favourite – alienation. The three verses depict various instances – the man who feels "soft in the middle [though] the rest of my life is so hard"; the man who, having lost his wife, his family, and his role-model, finds "my nights are so long"; the man lost in "a street in a strange world".

Now, though, merely depicting social alienation is not sufficient for the revitalised Simon. As in 'Graceland', he offers a redemption from such angst. This time it is not music but friendship which provides the means of salvation – "if you'll be my bodyguard I can be your long lost pal". A penny whistle solo by Morris Goldberg (a white South African based in New York) offers plaintive support to the music of Baghiti Khumalo and Ray Phiri, underlining the fragility of human relationships which Simon so frequently sees and so sympathetically describes.

'Al' was a number four hit in the UK, helped by an unusual, slightly surreal, video whose principal attraction was its stark simplicity in the age of big budget, often pretentious, rock videos. Shot with one stationary camera on one simple set, it featured Simon's friend, the actor Chevy Chase, appearing as Simon, playing a bass guitar, while Simon himself appears dressed similarly in the same location, almost as a guest in his own video.

UNDER AFRICAN SKIES

If 'Graceland' offers the *possibility* of redemption through music, then the subject of 'Under African Skies' is its achievement – "after the dream of falling and calling your name out, these are the roots of rhythm and the roots of rhythm remain".

Set to a lilting 'walking rhythm' and backed by Linda Ronstadt's beautiful descant, which seems to echo to the very skies Simon sings about, the song opens and closes with a pen-portrait of 'Joseph' (a name undoubtedly suggested by that of his collaborator Joseph Shabalala but perhaps more accurately to be taken as symbolising an African Everyman). In a few deft lines, Simon sketches both man and continent. Listening to the words and the music together, it is impossible not to sense the vastness of the skies under which Joseph walks.

The middle verse, which shifts curiously from Simon's own, masculine, gender ("my nursery door") to the feminine half way through, contains his clearest statement of the redemptive power of music – "give her the wings to fly through harmony and she won't bother you no more".

HOMELESS

Co-written with Joseph Shabalala, the leader of Ladysmith Black Mambazo, 'Homeless' is unlike any of the other songs on the album. It is sung entirely a cappella, showcasing the remarkable

range and power of Shabalala's ensemble. The lyrics, alternating between Zulu and English, have no discernible narrative structure, consisting mainly of phrases rather than complete sentences. The theme, as we shall see, is African.

Simon has said that "[we] wrote in English and Zulu, starting the piece in the middle and working outwards to the beginning and end". The crux of the song, therefore, is the verse beginning "strong wind destroy our home, many dead tonight it could be you". This song is not about homelessness as a social problem affecting affluent Western societies (not least London, where the song was recorded at Abbey Road Studios). This is the homelessness of massacre victims in a society where political violence rages. The haunting power of the key repeated chorus "we are homeless... moonlight sleeping on a midnight lake" works not just literally but as a metaphor for the political dispossession of the black South African majority.

The song ends with a verse in Zulu which translates as: "We would like to announce to the entire nation that we are the best at singing in this style". What, in another context, might simply be an amusing piece of performers' egotism becomes a statement of defiance. We do not accept, Ladysmith Black Mambazo proclaim, the sub-human status to which our oppressors wish to condemn us. We do not merely deserve better – we are better.

CRAZY LOVE, VOL. II

With 'Crazy Love, Vol. II' Simon reverts to the music and the themes that dominate the album. Guitarist Ray Phiri's band Stimela provide the backing for the interwoven stories of Fat Charlie and the singer, both of whom seem to be in the throes (*sic*) of divorce. (It may be conjectured that this is the "second volume" of the title, divorce being an established stage in the life-cycle of American love affairs.)

The chorus lines ("I don't want no part ..."), repeated with subtle rhythmic variation after each of the song's three

verses, shows Simon rejecting the "craziness" of a life "on fire ... all over the evening news" and telling his ex that this time "the joke is on her".

Initially recorded in the Ovation Studios in Johannesburg, the song was completed at the Hit Factory in New York. Morris Goldberg, the penny whistler on 'You Can Call Me Al', makes another appearance, this time on soprano sax.

THAT WAS YOUR MOTHER

As if to make the point that this is a Paul Simon album, not a World Music curiosity, *Graceland* ends with two songs rooted in specifically American musical traditions. The first of these was recorded in Louisiana with backing from those doyens of the Cajun scene Good Rockin' Dopsie & The Twisters.

Opening with the robust accordion of the great Dopsie himself (Alton Rubin Sr), and thus linking the song to the Gumboots accordion-based style which originally inspired the album, 'That Was Your Mother' is a jolly romp, sung by a father to his (implicitly grown-up) son, recalling the circumstances in which the son's parents met. The singer reminds his son (whom he loves, despite his being "the burden of my generation" – a pun Simon uses to great poetic effect) that, though he might now be a parental authority figure, he was once a young man "standing on the corner of Lafayette" looking for some action. It is an observation few children relish hearing or are capable of fully understanding.

It is a mark of Simon's maturity that he can use this subject, and in a song of such danceable brio. (Irony is added by the presence in The Twisters' line-up of two of Dopsie's own sons). It is also remarkable that, in such a seemingly simple song, he simultaneously takes the "child's" position *vis à vis* a musical "parent" and pays homage to Clifton Chenier, founding father of Cajun music and "the King of the Bayou".

ALL AROUND THE WORLD or THE MYTH OF FINGERPRINTS

The final song is perhaps the bleakest on the album. The second "American" track, this time backed by the Tex-Mex stars Los Lobos, it also features the accordion – David Hildago establishing a rocking tempo which, with the long and beautiful "oo oo oo" vocal melody, belies the unvarnished grimness of the song's lyrical content.

If the chorus is melancholy (the sun getting first "weary" and then "bloody" before setting, the lack of any answer to the question "what's a better thing to do" in "the black pit town", and the universality of this condition "all around the world"), then the verses positively drip with ennui. The first verse, in the voice of the cynical, faded "former talk-show host", defines "the myth of fingerprints" – far from being unique, as criminologists affirm, "I've seen them all and man they're all the same". The second verse uses the image of an army post – that it is abandoned only adds to the world-weary tone – as a classic example of the crushing of individuality, in this case of the army's new recruits. The third verse largely repeats the first but, with no need to repeat his definition of the myth, Simon ends with a bleak conclusion – "that's why we must learn to live alone".

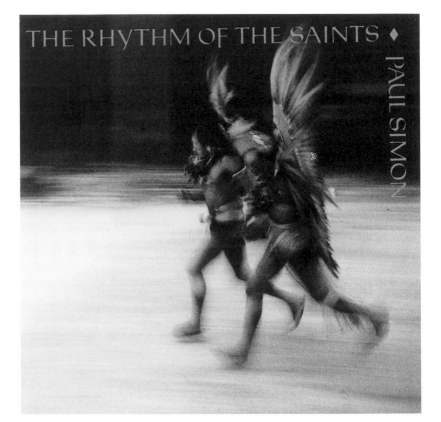

THE RHYTHM OF THE SAINTS

WARNER BROS 9 26098-2, SEPTEMBER 1990

Following Graceland was never going to be easy and, sensibly, Simon elected not to try. *The Rhythm Of The Saints*, recorded largely in Brazil, was a far more low-key enterprise, free from the drama – on and off the record – that surrounded the release of its predecessor.

As the title implies, *The Rhythm Of The Saints* is rhythm based, its principal focus the tuned drums and delicate percussion to be found in parts of South America, or more specifically, in Simon's case, in Salvador, Brazil. The result is an album of far gentler pace than *Graceland*, though some small degree of unity is sustained by Vincent Nguini's electric guitar which floats in and out of the percussive grooves much like Ray Phiri's guitar on *Graceland*, its smooth, undulating arpeggios drifting along like a coastal breeze.

Lacking the stylistic variety of *Graceland*, many of the songs on *The Rhythm Of the Saints* sound very similar, even after repeated listening. Which isn't to suggest that the album is dull – far from it – just that instead of switching gears to sustain interest, Simon has chosen to establish a mood which is more or less maintained throughout. As a result it's possible to drift in and out of the danceable grooves as each song tumbles into the next and lose track of things... as if subconsciously Simon is somehow recalling the *laissez-faire* attitude of life in the tropics where in a sun drenched climate, mañana is always preferable to bustling along.

In an industry where the vast majority of performers settle for what they know their fans want, much credit is due to Simon for continuing his quest for something different. South American music, of course, is not nearly so unfamiliar to the world at large as South African music, and this fact alone renders *The Rhythm Of The Saints* less startling than

Graceland. Nevertheless, instead of taking the usual samba or bossa nova-like approach of most American pop performers, Simon again develops a sound that is largely unique, balancing the rhythms of Brazil with his own Americanised recording style, as in 'Can't Run But' where the percussive pitter-patter of the native musicians is pitched against guitarist J.J. Cale's spicy, understated blues.

Emphasising this mood, the lyrics throughout are as elusive as any in Simon's catalogue. There's a vague thread of struggle, perhaps inspired by the appalling poverty in Brazil, and coming to terms with one's lot, and of travelling, but it's hard to pinpoint where Simon's thoughts are headed. The lyrics are slippery and at times surreal, and a line that makes literal sense is often followed by a line that appears solely to have been written because it fits securely into the groove, a smooth course of wordplay that seems more concerned with the rhythms established by these skilled percussionists

than making any literal sense.

In the UK *The Rhythm Of The Saints* shot up to no 1 and lingered in the charts for 28 weeks. In the US it reached no 4, staying in the Top 200 for 53 weeks and selling just over two million, about half as many as its predecessor.

THE OBVIOUS CHILD

The sharp rat-tat-tat of the Brazilian drums that open and close this song — and the shows that Simon performed after its release — set the tone for the entire album. Here, the percussionists, Grupo Cultural Olodum, were recorded live outdoors in Pelourinho Square in Salvador, and their insistent rhythms dominate throughout, the only respite coming from Michael Brecker's sinuous EWI synthesiser.

The lyrics address the struggle to survive, and there's a flashback to Simon's ever-present attention to detail in the gentle refrain as 'Sonny' looks through his old school yearbook, recalling his school friends and musing on the different ways in which their lives have evolved.

As a single in the UK, 'The Obvious Child' reached no 15.

CAN'T RUN BUT

Recorded largely in Brazil, the harmonically attractive tuned percussion establishes an insistent shuffle tempo behind a melody line and tone that is not entirely unlike one of the strands in Mike Oldfield's *Tubular Bells*. Appropriately, Simon is joined by the master of understated shuffle guitar, J.J. Cale, though his bluesy licks are far from conspicuous.

Lyrically, the song opens with some perceptive comments on the need to protect the earth's ecology from industrialisation, but the slipperiness of the sentiments have twisted and turned like the muddy river by the time the third verse comes around. Here Simon draws a parallel between the ravages of the planet and the way in which the spirit of rock –

the spirit that inspired him in the first place – seems to have deteriorated during his lifetime, commenting pithily that 'The music suffers/The music business survives'.

THE COAST

A lovely, flowing rhythm track establishes the foundation for guitarist Vincent Nguini's lightning arpeggios, and as the music glides along there are echoes of the swaying grooves that dominated *Graceland*.

The song tells of a journey undertaken by a family of musicians, possibly busking their way along the "injured coast". A vocal *tour-de-force*, especially on the concluding verse, Simon's own voice is enhanced by the ultra-smooth backing vocals of his friends Ladysmith Black Mambazo alongside Karen Bernód, Myra Lynn Gomila and Kia Jeffries.

PROOF

A bright, breezy rhythm track, again dominated by chattering tuned percussion, circles around plucked and dampened guitar strings, punctuated by sharp, stabbing brass lines. Against this, Simon leads his quartet of female backing singers through a song about the relentless struggle to overcomes lowly beginnings and better oneself elsewhere. Proof, he declares, is the "bottom line for everyone" along this particular journey.

FURTHER TO FLY

Tuned drums offer a variety of unusual percussive effects pitched against another insistent rhythm track. Over this Simon sings a series of elusive lyrics which again suggest that overcoming life's problems, and keeping your strength up despite disappointments, is purely a matter of will power.

The noted keyboard player Greg Phillinganes plays some airy synthesiser, alongside Michael Brecker's solos on EWI, his wind-driven synth controller.

SHE MOVES ON

After a percussive intro and occasional slapped bass, *Graceland* guitarist Ray Phirigives the track a similar ambience to the African songs on Simon's previous album. Amid yet another wide range of percussive effects, Simon sings of a fantasy woman, an unattainable lover who moves on like the wind, leaving him weak, though in the end, as her plane heads for the sky, there's also a sense of relief. The quartet of female backing singers offer a nice contrast to Simon's more precise diction.

BORN AT THE RIGHT TIME

'Born At The Right Time' boasts one of the strongest melodies on *Rhythm Of The Saints*, and it seems surprising that it wasn't selected as a single to introduce the album, though at this stage in his career no-one at Simon's record

label would have been under any illusion that he was likely to set the singles charts alight on either side of the Atlantic. The world tour that followed the release of *The Rhythm Of The Saints* was called the 'Born At The Right Time Tour' which surely reflects Simon's own fondness for the song.

The recurring guitar riff is faintly reminiscent of the Sun Records rockabilly style that occurs in much of Simon's catchiest work. There's a wealth of things happening deep within the mix, including bottles and bells and Clifton's Chenier's accordion, and the backing singers enhance beautifully Simon's own vocals, especially on the choruses.

The lyrics concern themselves with the population explosion, Simon having doubtless been inspired by the critical proportions that this problem has reached in Brazil. "The planet groans each time it registers another birth," he sings, though the specific subject of Simon's theme seems to have been born into the kind of nurturing circumstances that are unlikely to be found in the shanty towns on the hillsides overlooking Rio de Janeiro.

THE COOL, COOL RIVER

Opening with a sustained shuffle rhythm, Simon's vocals seem deliberately under-sung on a less tuneful song than most which borders on the monotonous and only reaches out when the brass ventures forth. The lyrics address the truism that no matter what may occur to mankind, the river keeps on flowing and always will. Probably the weakest song on the album.

SPIRIT VOICES

Vincent Nguini's slinky guitar arpeggios re-introduce the album's melodic flow on this attractive, peaceful journey song. The bustle of the Brazilian drums again dominates the rhythm, and Simon is joined on vocals by Milton Nascimento whose Portuguese lyrics are sung in counterpoint to Simon's English. The sleepy ambience and calm assurance of the guitar playing makes this one of the most pleasing tracks on the album.

THE RHYTHM OF THE SAINTS

The album concludes, as it began, with the pitter-patter of drums, joined at times by a shimmering, shaken percussion effect. Not inappropriately, in view of the album's overall theme of overcoming hardships, the lyrics of the title track take the form of a prayer, seeking help in overcoming obstacles and dominating the impossible.

Again percussion based, the melody is hustled along by three guitars, accordion and the strangely named Biana guitar of Armando Macedo.

PAUL SIMON IN CONCERT
LIVE RHYMIN'

WITH URUBAMBA
AND THE
JESSY DIXON SINGERS

LIVE ALBUMS

LIVE RHYMIN'

CBS 69059/WARNER BROS 25590 MARCH 1974

Simon's first live album was an understated affair recorded on his first solo tour during 1973. At this early stage in his solo career, he was obviously in no hurry to shake off his past and the album includes no fewer than six Simon & Garfunkel songs, together with five from his first two solo albums, plus one song by The Jesse Dixon Group alone.

Produced and engineered by Phil Ramone, the recording quality is excellent throughout. Indeed, so quiet are the audience and so precise are the solo performances that at times it is difficult to remember that this is a live recording.

Simon opens the show alone with a rousing version of 'Me And Julio Down By The Schoolyard' on which, as ever, his rhythm guitar work is impeccable. Two slower songs, 'Homeward Bound' and 'American Tune', follow, and the latter benefits from its stark, precise accompaniment. Simon is then joined by Urubamba, the South American group, for 'El Condor Pasa (If I Could)',

'Duncan' and 'The Boxer', on which the extra verse is heard for the first time. All three songs benefit from the spicy South American instrumentation.

Aside from the final encore of 'America', the Jesse Dixon group join Simon for the remainder of the album. 'Mother And Child Reunion' loses some of its reggae feel amid their gospel treatment, but the full choral accompaniment on 'The Sound Of Silence' offers a piquant alternative to the original. The most dramatic reworking, though, is on 'Bridge Over Troubled Water', now a full throated *tour de force*, extended to over seven minutes, and featuring a call and response section in which the lines "I will ease your mind" are repeated many times. Though the original melody is intact, this radical re-arrangement was a bold move for Simon to make on a song as universally popular as 'Bridge...'. The audience, who might have been expected to prefer the original, certainly liked it, even though a slightly tetchy Art Garfunkel was later quoted as saying that he preferred the S&G version on the album of the same name.

Simon hands the stage over to the Dixon band for 'Jesus Is The Answer', then returns for a rousing 'Loves Me Like A Rock'. Finally, as an encore, Simon offers an exquisite and very precise rendering of 'America' but not before the audience cry out for him to... "Say a few words". Clearly unprepared, he states: "Let's hope we all continue to live...", cutting off, apparently in mid-sentence and, in best Paul Simon fashion, appearing slightly enigmatic. He would repeat the exact phrase on other occasions.

In the US *Live Rhymin'* reached only

a disappointing number 33 in the charts, although it earned a Gold Disc. In the UK it failed to make the LP charts. Somewhat disappointingly, the packaging failed to fully credit the backing musicians, an oversight that remains uncorrected on subsequent CD pressings of the album. This is all the more surprising considering Simon's generous acknowledgement during the concert itself.

Full track listing: 'Me And Julio Down By The Schoolyard', 'Homeward Bound', 'American Tune', 'El Condor Pasa', 'Duncan', 'The Boxer', 'Mother And Child Reunion', 'The Sound Of Silence', 'Jesus Is The Answer', 'Bridge Over Troubled Water', 'Loves Me Like A Rock', 'America'.

SIMON AND
GARFUNKEL

THE CONCERT
IN CENTRAL PARK

THE CONCERT IN CENTRAL PARK

GEFFEN GEF 96008/WARNER BROS 3654   MARCH 1982

Simon & Garfunkel reunited in the summer of 1981 for a concert in New York's Central Park to raise money for the city. Although it seemed from the stage – and from the music – that the old friends had mellowed and were once again the best of friends, behind the scenes the rehearsals were by all accounts fraught with tension.

Garfunkel had proposed that a Simon & Garfunkel reunion should be exactly that: Simon & Garfunkel on stage together as they were in the Sixties, without any other musicians to clutter up the proceedings. Simon, on the other hand, felt that the music he'd recorded since the duo's break-up was written with a band in mind, and a band was needed to reproduce it on stage. Also, he was wary about having to play guitar for over two hours as their sole accompaniment, especially since he'd only recently managed to overcome the problem of calcium deposits on his fingers. One solution was that Simon should open the show with a band and the second half be devoted to S&G, but this placed Simon in the awkward position of having to open for Simon & Garfunkel. In the end Garfunkel backed down, but the tension lingered.

Such misgivings were forgotten on the day of the show, and the duo delivered all that was expected of them to the delight of a crowd estimated at half a million. Although the singing and playing lacks the absolute precision of the music on either Simon's own 1974 live album or his concert in Central Park in August 1991, which was also recorded, the atmosphere of the night comes across and makes up for any slight raggedness in the performance.

Introduced by New York Mayor Ed Koch, who'd been instrumental in helping to organise the event, Simon & Garfunkel launch straight into a loose but spirited 'Mrs Robinson' with Steve Gadd's drums setting a strict tempo. "It's great to do a neighbourhood concert," announces Simon three songs in. After thanking various officials, he wins over the crowd by announcing, unlikely as it might seem, that the guys selling loose joints are giving half their income to good causes.

The most interesting aspect of the concert was hearing Garfunkel's harmonic touch on songs recorded by Simon alone. He certainly seems at home on 'Me And Julio Down By The Schoolyard', which is enhanced by a lively saxophone solo from Gerry Niewood and is the first of seven Simon solo songs that appear on the live recording. Garfunkel also adds his voice to 'American Tune', 'Slip Sliding Away' and 'Kodachrome' while Simon tackles 'Still Crazy After All These Years, 'Late In The Evening' and '50 Ways To Leave Your Lover' without his former partner. On the night he also performed what

was then a very new song, 'The Late Great Johnny Ace', his tribute to John Lennon, but this does not appear on the record, perhaps because he was interrupted by a member of the audience climbing on stage, apparently with the intention of talking to Simon. In view of the song he was singing, it was, by all accounts, a very tense moment.

There are many high points on this record, many of them provided by the band. David Brown's closing guitar solo on 'America' is outstanding, drummer Steve Gadd is excellent throughout, especially on the pacey numbers like 'Wake Up Little Susie', 'Late In The Evening' and the 'Kodachrome/ 'Maybelline' medley, and on '50 Ways To Leave Your Lover', he replicates the tricky march time tempo of the original beat for beat. Indeed, such is the proficiency of the 11-piece band that Simon's insistence on their presence is more than fully justified.

Inevitably, Garfunkel shines on a note perfect 'Bridge Over Troubled Water', performed here as it was recorded, with Richard Tee on piano, and he's given a solo spot with the appropriately popular 'A Heart In New York' from his upcoming *Scissors Cut* album. The best duo performance is probably 'The Boxer', where Simon & Garfunkel's voices blend perfectly on one of Simon's finest songs. The crowd reaction to the additional verse is especially touching. This ought to have been the climax to the evening: the duo-only 'Old Friends', '59th Street Bridge Song' and 'Sounds Of Silence' which follow seem strangely anti-climactic.

"Afterwards our first reaction was, I think, one of disappointment," Simon said later, "Arthur's more than mine. He thought he didn't sing well. I didn't get what had happened, how big it was, until I went home, turned on the television and saw it on the news, the people being interviewed, and later that night, on the front pages of all the newspapers. Then I got it."

When the dust had settled Simon & Garfunkel took roughly the same show on the road, first to Europe, then the

Antipodes, then the USA. It was not a happy tour. Tensions flared up in Europe and lingered elsewhere, reviews were mixed and, when it was all over, neither party wanted to repeat the experience.

The *Central Park* album attracted fine reviews. *Rolling Stone*: "The new album has magic to spare, some of it rough. Though laboured over in the studio after the event, the tracks are far from 100 per cent polished. It's actually refreshing. If *The Concert In Central Park* is Paul Simon's Valentine to the Big Apple, it is Art Garfunkel's voice that really tugs at the heartstrings and sends the message home."

The Concert In Central Park reached number 6 in both the US and UK album charts. It is now available as a single CD.

Full track listing: 'Mrs Robinson', 'Homeward Bound', 'America', 'Me And Julio Down By The Schoolyard', 'Scarborough Fair', 'April Come She Will', 'Wake Up Little Susie', 'Still Crazy After All These Years', 'American Tune', 'Late In the Evening', 'Slip Slidin' Away', 'A Heart In New York', 'Kodachrome/Maybelline', 'Bridge Over Troubled Water', '50 Ways To Leave Your Lover', 'The Boxer', 'Old Friends', 'The 59th Street Bridge Song (Feelin' Groovy)', 'The Sounds Of Silence'.

Paul Simon's

Concert In The Park

August 15th, 1991

PAUL SIMON'S CONCERT IN THE PARK

WARNER BROS 26737 NOVEMBER 1991

From the snap, crackle and pop of the drum fanfare to the mellifluous beauty of the loveliest version of 'Sounds Of Silence' you'll find anywhere, *Paul Simon's Concert In The Park* is the (double) album to own if you want only one Paul Simon album on your shelf. The whole enterprise serves to make the earlier Simon & Garfunkel *Concert In Central Park* album seem almost shoddy in comparison.

This time around Simon took no chances and his meticulous attention to detail shines out in the re-arrangements of almost every song. Concentrating on material from *Graceland* and *Rhythm Of The Saints*, Simon recruited many of the musicians that appeared on these albums, including no fewer than four additional percussionists plus the now familiar figure of Steve Gadd, widely regarded as the foremost session drummer in the world. As if these weren't enough, Simon is joined on the opening track by Grupo Cultural Olodum from Brazil, and the massed army of drummers herald the beginning of the show with a shot of rhythm that jolts the senses and seems designed to eradicate finally and forever the 'formerly of Simon & Garfunkel' tag that stuck so stubbornly for so long.

Simon offers 11 songs from his two most recent albums, seven from his earlier solo albums and five, including the final four, from the S&G era. The emphasis on the newer work offers ample opportunity for the Third World musicians to demonstrate their chops and prominent throughout are the three guitarists, Vincent Nguini, Ray Phiri and John Selolwane, and the remarkable bass playing of Armand Sabal-Lecco. The clerkly Michael Brecker, who has come to bear a striking resemblance to Glen

Miller as he grows older, frequently steps forward to solo on saxophone and EWI, the wind-driven synthesiser.

The full band renditions of the four closing S&G numbers are most impressive, with 'Cecilia' in particular benefiting from an extraordinary rearrangement. Finally, returning to the Central Park stage to welcome back his old friend the darkness yet again, Paul glides through the melody of his oldest hit on electric guitar before offering a particularly reflective interpretation of the lyrics. Naturally, the line about "10,000 people, maybe more," raises a huge cheer, but the highlight of this version is the superbly eloquent guitar solo by Ray Phiri. The song has never sounded better.

Recorded on August 15, 1991, in the UK *Paul Simon's Concert In Central Park* reached only a disappointing number 60, staying in the charts for just one week. It deserved far better.

Full track listing: 'The Obvious Child', 'The Boy In The Bubble', 'She Moves On', 'Kodachrome', 'Born At the Right Time', 'Train In The Distance', 'Me And Julio Down By The Schoolyard', 'I Know What I Know', 'The Cool Cool River', 'Bridge Over Troubled Water', 'Proof', 'The Coast', 'Graceland', 'You Can Call Me Al', 'Still Crazy After All These Years', 'Loves Me Like A Rock', 'Diamonds On The Soles Of Her Shoes', 'Hearts And Bones', 'Late In The Evening', 'America', 'The Boxer', 'Cecilia', 'The Sound Of Silence'.

SIMON AND GARFUNKEL'S GREATEST HITS

Bridge Over Troubled Water
Mrs. Robinson
The Sound Of Silence
The Boxer
The 59th Street Bridge Song
(Feelin' Groovy)
Scarborough Fair / Canticle
I Am A Rock
Kathy's Song
Cecilia
America
Bookends
Homeward Bound
El Condor Pasa
(If I Could)
For Emily,
Whenever
I May Find Her

Stereo

COMPILATIONS

Although it wasn't until 1972 when the first Simon & Garfunkel Greatest Hits album was released, there has been a steady proliferation of compilation albums for both S&G and Simon himself ever since. At least two substantial Simon & Garfunkel collections on a single CD are currently available, as is an imported 3 CD Collected Works anthology (Columbia C3K 45322) which brings together all their recordings from *Wednesday Morning, 3AM* through to *Bridge Over Troubled Water* at a somewhat pricey £55.99.

Also available, somewhat curiously, is a three album boxed package containing *Sounds Of Silence*, *The Graduate* soundtrack and *Bridge Over Troubled Water*, priced at £21.49.

SIMON AND GARFUNKEL'S GREATEST HITS
CBS 69003/COLUMBIA 31950 JULY 1972

The first Simon & Garfunkel hits collection was a huge success, staying on the US charts for over two years and in the UK for even longer – a massive 281 weeks. It comprised a generous 14, tracks, including a previously unissued live version of 'America'. Chronological sequencing would have improved the set.

Full track listing: 'Mrs Robinson', 'For Emily, Whenever I May Find Her', 'The Boxer', 'The 59th Street Bridge Song', 'The Sound Of Silence', 'I Am A Rock', 'Scarborough Fair/Canticle', 'Homeward Bound', 'Bridge Over Troubled Water', 'America', 'Kathy's Song', 'El Condor Pasa', 'Bookends', 'Cecilia'.

THE SIMON AND GARFUNKEL COLLECTION

CBS 10029/COLUMBIA 45322
NOVEMBER 1981

This improved, expanded collection reached number 4 in the UK, staying on the charts for 80 weeks. It still wasn't sequenced chronologically but it offered a broader sweep than the previous compilation. The cover picture of 'Simon & Garfunkel' walking along a beach together seems to have been posed by models who resemble Paul and Art rather than the real thing!

Full track listing: 'I Am A Rock', 'Homeward Bound', 'America', 'The 59th Street Bridge Song', 'Wednesday Morning, 3AM', 'El Condor Pasa', 'At The Zoo', 'Scarborough Fair/Canticle', 'The Boxer', 'Sound Of Silence', 'Mrs Robinson', 'Keep The Customer Satisfied', 'Song For The Asking', 'Hazy Shade Of Winter', 'Cecilia', 'Old Friends/Bookends Theme', 'Bridge Over Troubled Water'.

THE DEFINITIVE SIMON & GARFUNKEL

SONY MOOD 21, NOVEMBER 1991

Another decade, another compilation, this one further expanded. There is talk of a substantial Simon & Garfunkel box set in the future, Simon's own box set having failed lamentably in presenting a true picture of their years together (see below). Until it does, this single CD set, finally in chronological order, is the best bet.

Full track listing: 'Wednesday Morning, 3AM', 'The Sound Of Silence', 'Homeward Bound', 'Kathy's Song', 'I Am A Rock', 'For Emily, Wherever I May Find Her', 'Scarborough Fair/Canticle', 'The 59th Street Bridge Song', 'Seven O'Clock News/Silent Night', 'A Hazy Shade Of Winter', 'El Condor Pasa (If I Could)', 'Mrs Robinson', 'America', 'At The Zoo', 'Old Friends', 'Bookends Theme', 'Cecilia', 'The Boxer', 'Bridge Over Troubled Water', 'Song For The Asking'.

GREATEST HITS, ETC

CBS 86047/COLUMBIA 35032 NOVEMBER1977

Paul Simon's first 'solo' compilation seemed somewhat premature after only three albums and a handful of 'hits', which is probably why the 'Etc' was added to the title. Simon's picture on the front, and the brown tints that surround it, are so sombre that they suggest a classical album by a classical artist.

In the US it reached no 9 and in the UK no 15.

It contained two songs that had not previously been released:

SLIP SLIDIN' AWAY

The first of the two seems to echo the common dream experience of never quite being able to reach your goal... "the nearer your destination, the more you're slip sliding away". More specifically, as ever with Simon, the song is about relationships, with the first verse describing an unrequited sexual longing, the second a relationship on the rocks and the third, possibly autobio-graphical, about a father trying to communicate with his son after divorcing the mother.

The lyrical enigma is etched into smooth, catchy melody, and is enhanced by backing vocals from The Oak Ridge Boys.

STRANDED IN A LIMOUSINE

The second otherwise unavailable song is a hard rhythmic piece based on a tale of how a gangster is spotted in his car, stopped at traffic lights. In another fine example of Simon's exquisite attention to detail, bystanders discuss shopping the villain to the police and sharing out the reward money but they are too late... before they know it the gangster has slipped out of their orbit, shedding his skin like a rattlesnake.

The stimulating horn arrangement was written by Simon and features Randy and Michael Brecker and David Sanborn, amongst others.

The remaining songs on this compilation are: 'Still Crazy After All These

Years', 'Have A Good Time', 'Duncan', 'Me And Julio Down By The Schoolyard', 'Something So Right', 'Kodachrome', 'I Do It For Your Love', '50 Ways To Leave Your Lover', 'American Tune', 'Mother And Child Reunion', 'Loves Me Like A Rock', 'Take Me To The Mardi Gras'.

NEGOTIATIONS AND LOVE SONGS (1971-1986)

WARNER BROS WX 223/WARNER BROS 25789
OCTOBER 1988

Eleven years separated the release of Simon's last compilation and this collection which was intended to replace and up-date the previous compilation, *Greatest Hits Etc*, which had long since been deleted. The new compilation included more recent material from *Hearts And Bones* and *Graceland*.

Nothing new appeared on this collection, which remains the basic 'Best Of...' album for those investigating Paul Simon's solo years who want to spend around £15 on a CD.

Tracks are: 'Mother And Child Reunion', 'Me And Julio Down By the Schoolyard', 'Something So Right', 'St Judy's Comet', 'Loves Me Like A Rock', 'Have A Good Time', 50 Ways To Leave Your Lover', 'Still Crazy After All These Years', 'Late In the Evening', 'Slip Slidin' Away', 'Hearts And Bones', 'Train In The Distance', 'Renée And Georgette Magritte With Their Dog After The War', 'Diamonds On The Soles Of Her Shoes', 'You Can Call Me Al', 'Graceland' (LP only), 'Kodachrome'.

Paul Simon
1964/1993

BOX SET

PAUL SIMON 1964-1993
WARNER BROS 9 45394-2

Paul Simon being the perfectionist that he is, it was never likely that his box set would reveal very much about his working methods or even contain unreleased demos or 'work in progress' material that wasn't perfect in every way. In the event, the three CD set included only one demo, for 'Bridge Over Troubled Water, and for many fans was a profound disappointment. It failed to convey anything like the scope of his career, largely because the third CD consisted almost entirely of selections, some of them live, from *Graceland* and *Rhythm Of The Saints*, his two most recent albums, while Simon & Garfunkel appeared on just 13 of the total of 52 tracks.

This could have been remedied by extending the package to four CDs and including more early material, especially songs from *Wednesday Morning*, which was overlooked completely, and *The Paul Simon Songbook*, which merited just one song. Instead, the box set appeared very much like a promotional tool for Simon's most recent work.

Such early favourites as 'I Am A Rock', 'The 59th Street Bridge Song', 'Scarborough Fair/Canticle', 'For Emily Wherever I May Find Her', 'Dangling Conversation' and even 'Homeward Bound' are absent. Curiously 'Hey Schoolgirl', Tom and Jerry's first ever effort, is located not at the very beginning of the set, where it belongs, but midway between the S&G tracks and Simon's solo work. Other previously unreleased material includes 'Thelma', a track that sounds like an outtake from *The Rhythm Of The Saints*, and *The Break-Up,* a quite hilarious conversation piece in which Paul and Artie discuss the break-up of Simon & Garfunkel.

The set included a booklet with two flattering essays on Simon's music, as well as comments from him on various songs.

CD 1 – 'Leaves That Are Green', 'The Sound Of Silence', 'Kathy's Song', 'America', 'Cecilia', 'El Condor Pasa', 'The Boxer', 'Mrs Robinson', 'Bridge Over Troubled Water' (demo), 'Bridge Over Troubled Water', 'The Breakup', 'Hey Schoolgirl', 'My Little Town', 'Me And Julio Down By The Schoolyard', 'Peace Like A River', 'Mother And Child Reunion', 'Congratulations', 'Duncan', 'American Tune'.

CD 2– 'Loves Me Like A Rock', 'Tenderness', 'Kodachrome', 'Gone At Last', 'Take Me To The Mardi Gras', 'St Judy's Comet', 'Something So Right', 'Still Crazy After All These Years', 'Have A Good Time', 'Jonah', 'How The Heart Approaches What It Yearns', '50 Ways To Leave Your Lover', 'Slip Slidin' Away', 'Late In The Evening', 'Hearts And Bones', 'Renée And Georgette Magritte With Their Dog After The War', 'The Late Great Johnny Ace'.

CD 3 – 'The Boy In The Bubble', 'Graceland', 'Under African Skies', 'That Was Your Mother', 'Diamonds On The Soles Of Her Shoes', 'You Can Call Me Al', 'Homeless', 'Spirit Voices', 'The Obvious Child', 'Can't Run But', 'Thelma', 'Further To Fly', 'She Moves On', 'Born At the Right Time', 'The Cool, Cool River', 'The Sound Of Silence'.

Finally, The Paul Simon Anthology (Warner Brothers 9362-45408-2), released shortly after the box set, brings together 36 tracks, including six Simon & Garfunkel recordings, in a reduced 2 CD edition of the above boxed set. The second album in this package, similar to the third in the box, concentrates almost exclusively on material from *Graceland* and *The Rhythm Of The Saints*. CD One contains the S&G songs and a considerably reduced selection from the first five Paul Simon solo albums.

INDEX